COLORS OF CONSCIOUSNESS

COLORS OF CONSCIOUSNESS

TWENTY-FIVE SOUL PAINTINGS | VOL. 1

NICOLE C. HARP

After my dear mother's dementia diagnosis, I would notice her staring off, unaware. I would try to bring her back by redirecting her with stories of the past that brought her peace, but there came a time when that no longer worked. She had one foot in this world and one foot in the other.

At times, we tried to have conversations about heaven and spaciousness, but neither of us could find the words. So I gathered my oil paints and set an intention to speak through art. I moved and glided about using three shades of soft white, then mixed in four cool and calming shades of blue to create an openness, or entry point, on the canvas. I hung the painting where she tended to stare. When she was mentally "somewhere else," this allowed her to physically focus on the surface and feel the colors. The painting became an illusion of space that gave her emotional and visual calm, if only for a short time.

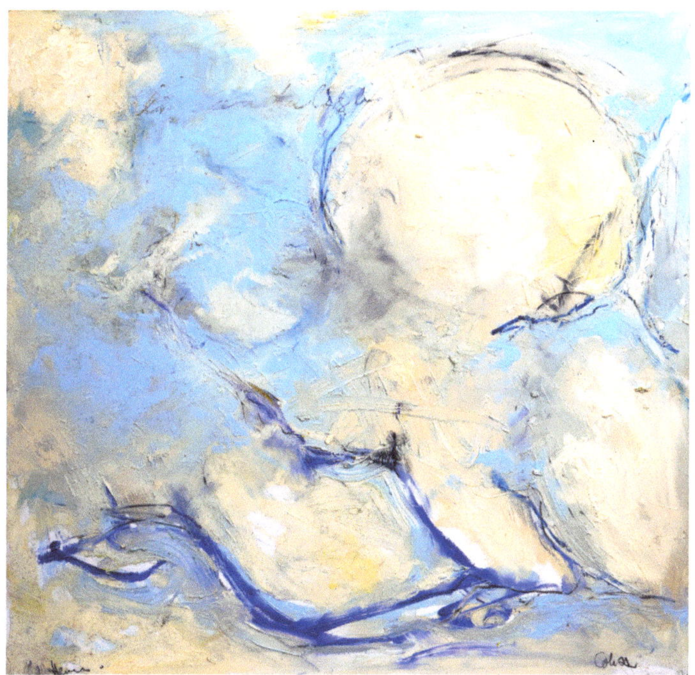

"To help her focus on something physical, all I could think to do, was to visually create a version of her heaven, a place for her to find focus and peace while moving between worlds."

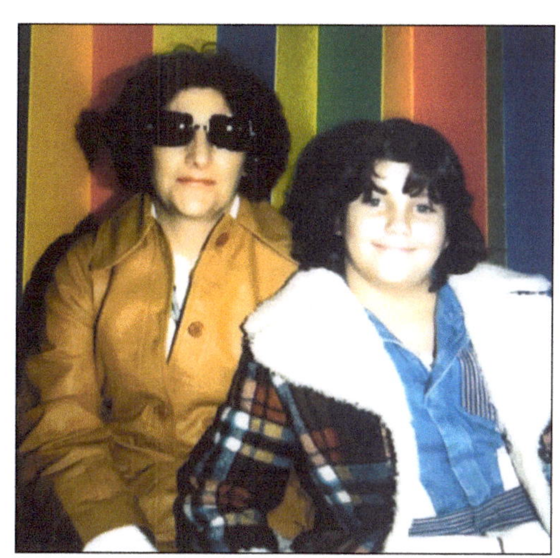

Praise For
COLORS OF CONSCIOUSNESS

"Starting with the riveting story of her mother's passage with dementia, Nicole's writing is full of feeling. Followed by the story of her artistic development, profound poems, and bright and lively soul paintings, you'll dive through the pages surrounded by a bubble bath of enrichment." —PENELOPE SMITH, FOUNDING PIONEER ANIMAL COMMUNICATOR, AUTHOR OF *ANIMAL TALK, WHEN ANIMALS SPEAK,* AND *ANIMALS IN SPIRIT* HTTPS://ANIMALTALK.NET/

"A stunning study of love and spirit and being human. Nicole captures the essence of what the hidden place inside of us knows, feels and yearns for, but lacks the refined senses to see. Spend time with this book and joy will arise within your heart and soul. I love this book!" —SHERRIE DILLARD AUTHOR *I'M STILL WITH YOU: COMMUNICATE, HEAL & EVOLVE WITH YOUR LOVED ONE ON THE OTHER SIDE*

"I deeply admire Nicole's ability to delve within and trust her higher power to guide her, it is truly inspiring. She captures the essence of the soul in her exquisite art works and eloquent words, creating a divine connection that resonates profoundly." —SHANNA VAVRA CREATOR OF *SENSE OF SOUL PODCAST*

"Nicole Harp's *Colors of Consciousness* breathes wisdom and kindness, her paintings and poems like arms stretched out to the stars, each pairing a prayer, an invitation for your soul to dance. Her ekphrastic works speak to compassion for fellow human beings, for the animals of the world, and for Mother Earth. Nicole writes that "love is waiting to be named," and this is where you, dear reader, will float away from this book with a desperate desire to hug your loved ones, speaking their names and your own." —EDDIE DOWE, AUTHOR OF *I HAVE TO TELL YOU SOMETHING* AND *NOTES FROM MY THERAPY SESSIONS*

"A touching and compelling story of unconditional love and compassion brought together with the elegant and stunning soul language of Nicole's extraordinary art. A masterful representation of a soul's journey and a gem you will undoubtedly come to cherish." —GEORGE TRIPODI, CONSULTANT AND ASTROLOGER

Table of Contents

How I Became a Soul Painter

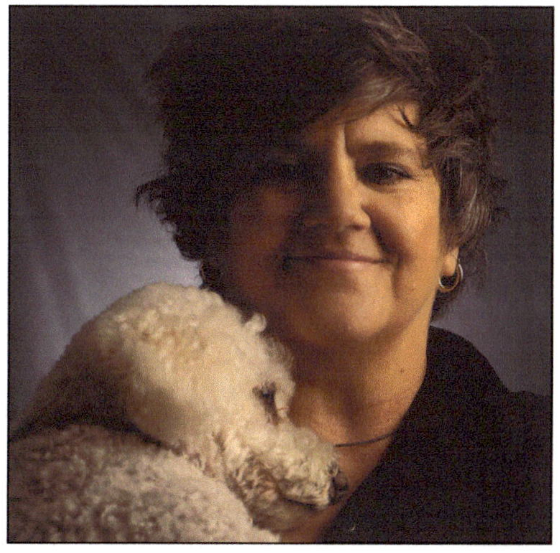

The impetus to connect with and paint twenty-five souls began with the soul that is most meaningful to me: the soul of my mother. I have been a professional abstract painter since 1992, with the majority of my artwork being academia-based. My training taught me to approach art from an intellectual, linear, and logical perspective, according to preestablished norms and rules. But my intuitive feelings were always guiding me in a truer, more aesthetic direction; one that embraced colors and textures and invited me to create from pure emotion and energy. In hindsight, I see how that was the beginning of my path to painting the soul and energy of animals and people. I was intuitively and energetically feeling souls while effortlessly communicating the subject's consciousness onto the painting surface.

Five years ago, I trained to become a professional intuitive and then professional animal communicator, building upon a lifetime of strong intuitive skills and innate abilities. As I began to open psychically and grow spiritually, I started receiving information from Spirit with a clarity I'd never experienced before. This work enabled me to be an open channel for energy to flow through me and onto the canvas.

The daily practice of meditation, of listening within to feel what colors and shapes should be expressed for each soul, was life-changing. I finally felt complete and was 100 percent in my body. This blissful feeling was an affirmation that I was fulfilling my calling, my destiny. I embodied being an abstract artist who interprets the consciousness of humans and animals in the physical and non-physical form. I could emotionally and energetically imprint energy onto canvas. This breakthrough coincided with my mother's illness, and things became clear. Everything I had done up until this point had prepared me for this moment.

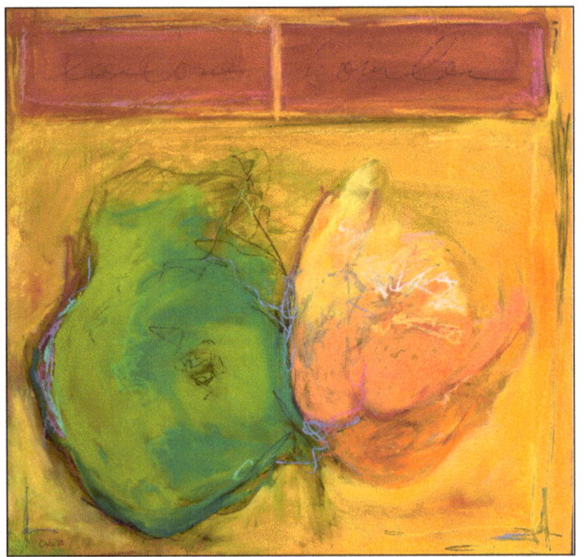

My Mother's Story

My mother's dementia diagnosis set into motion two years of intimately listening, watching, and experiencing all aspects of a person's soul. Eyes wide open, I navigated that time with my mother as she heroically walked through each stage of her disease.

As ugly as the disease of dementia is, it allowed for something beautiful to blossom between my mother and me: we were able to heal our relationship. The disease stripped away all of our old patterns and dysfunctions of communicating and relating to each other. It broke free the most honest and pure essence of our beings. We became the best parts of ourselves; the open-hearted souls we were born into this world to be.

This whirlwind of emotion evolved in challenging and surprising ways. For me, it was also a time of self-discovery and introspection. The uncovering had to do with what a soul is, how I can communicate with a soul, and what gifts a soul brings to its physical form. I was thrust into presence, the key to truly feeling and experiencing my life and connecting deeper with my mother.

Doris Carol Harp was born and raised on the Upper East Side in Manhattan, New York, in 1937. Raised by a single mother, Doris was the youngest of four. With fourteen years separating her from her closest sibling, it was like being an only child. Grit, determination, and resilience were necessary for her survival and successes. I know exactly where she got that resolve: my Nana, Viola Accetturo. Knowing her daughter was smart and would pass the entrance test, Nana marched down to St. Patrick's Cathedral, the all-girls private Catholic school, and got my mother enrolled. She was accepted on a sliding financial scale scholarship from elementary school through high school.

Proud of her Italian and French heritage, she knew the names and dates of stories dating back to Ellis Island. Doris was a true New Yorker, from her love of big band sounds like Frank Sinatra to her classic style and dress. She always said, "We wear black in New York until we can find something darker."

Divorced early in her marriage, she courageously raised my brother and me as a single parent. We are forever grateful for her selfless devotion and generosity. She spoke up for injustice, especially when it came to animals. Her love, compassion, and protection of animals was immense, and she surrounded herself with shelter or rescue animals her whole life. She cared deeply for her friends and was genuinely interested in listening and helping in whatever way she could.

Doris loved to sing and dance and was a lover of the arts. Her favorite painters were Edward Hopper and Wayne Thiebaud. But her favorite artist, whom she supported with all her heart, was me. When I was unsure about selecting a college major, she asked me what classes I enjoyed that didn't feel like work. Art was the resounding answer. My uncle had offered to pay my way if I majored in business, but my mom said we would find our own way, and we did. She often told me, "Ask for what you want, and the worst that can happen is they say no."

Doris had a beautiful soul. In the end, her brightest light shined through as sweet, gentle, sensitive, and This is how she will always be remembered: a beacon of light and love.

Our relationship was complex. Like a lot of mothers and daughters, it was loving yet challenging. I saw the best parts of myself in my mother; sometimes I could see the worst. We often butted heads over the silliest things. But on the hardcore beliefs about life, nature, goodness, and morality, we were simpatico. As it turns out, that was the most important element I needed to focus on—our deep connection.

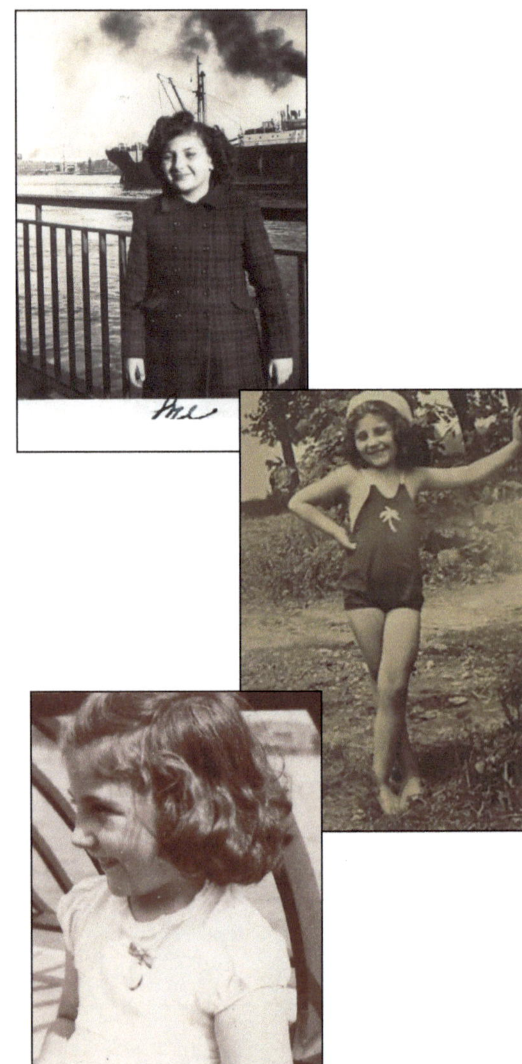

In hindsight, I wish I had been conscious enough at the time to cut her a break. I would have liked to have been there for her when I was younger, to share her grief from the loss of her mother and sisters. I wish I had been in touch with my pain enough to know and accept that crying and speaking of grief was an honorable way to navigate through it. I also wish our mother/daughter dynamic allowed for just that: for me to be a friend and for us to share the deepest parts of ourselves. I was not ready or able to know this. As a middle-age adult, I still was not ready.

With life experience comes awareness and inner growth. By understanding my mother, I now better understand myself. Looking at my mother was like looking into a mirror; her kindness, personality, and stubbornness were reflecting back at me.

The façade of humor and strength was just a cover-up for the immense pain she had experienced and never processed: a life filled with disappointment and regret. I began to notice that our core beliefs were what kept us tight; they were strong and resilient. We had an unspoken love and commitment that we would always be there for one another. We didn't say I love you a lot, but we showed it in every moment by our actions.

Perhaps it was a generational thing, but our family didn't speak of death, although I tried. We didn't ask for help, we didn't cry, and we didn't have a plan for my mother when she got older. So when she started to show signs of dementia, the only thing my spouse and I could think of was to move into a larger house so that my mother could live with us. My mother had been strong and independent her whole life. She really did do life on her own terms until her last breath.

We bought a house that would allow for all three of us to live and have space. The night before we were about to pack her up, my mother called, crying. She couldn't move in with us. She had come this far in life on her own and wanted to leave it that way. A deep part of me knew she was sparing us from what was coming: being the caretaker of a loved one with dementia. She did not want our house to become a nursing home twenty-four seven. She was being selfless, yet I didn't see it that way at first. I was trying to control a situation that was becoming so erratically out of control.

Getting creative with her assistance while I was at work was how Mom would remain safe. I decided to hire my friends on the down-low. I would say things like, "Mom, this is Anni. She's my friend from work who wanted to meet you and spend some time with you." Sometimes this would work; other times, it wouldn't. But any success we had was a major milestone. My mother had been calling the shots her entire life and never needed input from anyone. Yet now she found herself in uncharted territory. Her independence was being challenged daily, and she couldn't quite figure out how and why.

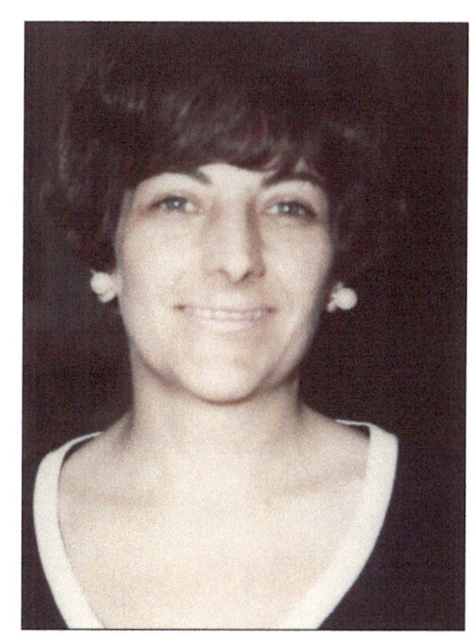

I became the adult who was forced to stand up, to say what was difficult, and to do the unthinkable just to make sure my mother was safe. The dementia had advanced to the stage where Mom was fighting to understand what was happening to her. One minute she knew how to lock the front door; the next moment she forgot where the keys were. Part of her knew what was happening. She could feel it deep inside but could not find the words to express her feelings. Other parts of her became frustrated. She would end up physically fighting with me and becoming combative. Sometimes she would walk out the front door for a stroll in her pajamas. Her actions varied. The days seemed endless.

It was clear at this point that my mom needed twenty-four-hour care. It was not enough anymore to have the daily visits, friends checking in on her, neighbors coming by to help with medicines and placing the phone back on the hook. The days of my mom balancing a checkbook to the penny with 100 percent accuracy were gone. Once meticulous and sharp, she had now become utterly baffled, confused, and out of control. She was happy one moment and sad the next. These were what our days consisted of now. Every day, all over again, my heart broke for her.

My mother was still refusing to leave her home. In her mind, she was fine, and we were the crazy ones. The fifth UTI was a godsend. It allowed her to be admitted to the hospital where she could receive full-time care. That night, when she left her home to go to the ER, was the last time she set foot in her house. After thirty-plus years, just like that, life as she knew it was forever changed. I would explain her tenuous situation to the nurses and doctors of how she was no longer safe at home without twenty-four-hour care.

It was heartbreaking how my spouse and I had to get up every day and continue to go to work. We could not physically care for my dear mother. This time, my heart broke wide open, filled with pain and disappointment in myself for not fulfilling an unrealistic promise of having my mother live with me into her old age. Instead, I had to visit nursing homes that were filled to capacity where patients sat slumped over in wheelchairs as they were pushed up and down long hallways and corridors. Agitated or emotionless, they sat patiently, waiting for anyone to come. My head was bursting with pressure at the reality of how my mother would spend her last months on this earth.

She was finally transferred to a permanent nursing home of our choice—after many months in a holding pattern and a long and laborious paperwork process. Along the way, what saved me and forced me to look deep inside myself with grace were the real angels on earth who came to our aid. People who were put on our path to guide us. People who made me realize the true depth of our humanity and goodness. People who truly live the life of service every day, despite the brutal caseloads, long hours, and low pay. They help because it is the right and caring thing to do. The ultimate human act is to love and care for all people like they are your family.

Roxanne from social services; Kathy from insurance; Indira, my mom's night nurse at the nursing home; and several more all served as angels on earth. I know with every fiber of my being that my mother and I could not have found peace during this exacerbation of the disease process without these souls mentoring us along our journey.

We got Mom set up in her room with everything we thought she could need. I tried to visit her as much as I could to make the transition as seamless as possible. Indira would call me most nights to let my mother and me hear each other's voices. We would talk about dinner, music, and how much hell my mom was giving Indira because she would not stop trying to get out of the wheelchair. My mother was a walker, restless when confined. She had already fallen five times while attempting to stand, not understanding she wasn't strong enough to do it unassisted. Always fiercely independent, resilient, and strong, I wondered why the disease seemed to change her essence.

Every day was an emotional roller coaster for her and for me. She would come in and out of lucidity. At times she would say, "What is happening to me? I can feel it. What's wrong with me? Why can't I remember?" Again, my heart shattered into a million pieces at the loss of my mother, both physically and mentally. On a very true and deep level, my mother knew what was happening to her. The person she knew herself to be was disappearing.

I promised myself to not worry about what I would say to her when I visited. I was determined to be present in the moment so I would not miss anything. I tried my best. Some days were more successful than others. What was there to say except to let my mother know I encouraged and supported her going to be with her family on the other side? I know she needed their love and comfort in a way I could not give her in this physical form.

I became my mother's advocate, which required a lot of confidence, willingness, and fortitude. She was the one who taught me how to be an advocate for myself, or for anyone who needed it. "Always speak up! Always ask!" she often said. As I felt her slipping away from my tender grasp, I learned to trust the universal rhythm of life itself. The juxtaposition of life and death, love and loss, holding on and letting go. Human emotions are shared human experiences. They are meaningful, complex, and, at times, unbearably painful.

A week and a day before Mother's Day, Amy came to visit Mom with me. We walked around outside, admiring the pretty flowers. Out of the blue, Mom threw a couple of sarcastic, quick-witted remarks at us. We laughed, but she didn't.

Then, in an instant, my mother looked disappointed, unable to know why and make it better. I was helpless again, and so was she. In silence, we soaked up all of the sun we could. Before we walked my mother back to the nursing home, she looked at me. In that instant, I knew. She had decided to start the final dying process. It was a feeling I had never felt before. It was strong and matter-of-fact. The unknown made me feel anxious, somewhat out of control, and unsure of when and how this process would unfold. I knew she was ready to let go.

This would be the last coherent visit with her. The following week I visited my mother every day after work, not really wanting to go home but needing to so I could sleep. I left each evening asking the universe to please let me know; please let me be there when she passes. If Indira hadn't been working as her night nurse, I might have slept in the chair next to her bed. But we did have her, and she called me those two nights as she always had. Indira sincerely cared about my mother and loved the essence of her sassy personality and wit.

Monday morning came, and when Indira and I spoke at four in the morning, she said, "Nicole, I think she is getting close." I had been debating whether or not to go to work, but the whole time I knew I couldn't. I was hesitating, acknowledging what I felt: today was the day my mother would pass over. I thought she was going to pass the day before, but that was Mother's Day, and I knew she would never let go on Mother's Day.

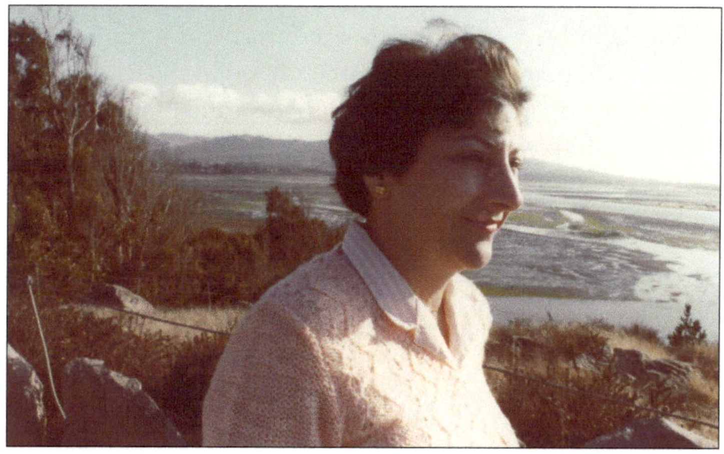

I threw on some clothes and hurriedly headed to the nursing home. What usually felt like a short trip to my mother's room suddenly felt like it was hours away. When I finally got there, standing in her room felt surreal. The seriousness and sacredness of this moment of waiting was indescribable. There was a palpable energy of love and loss that was momentous and deep.

My mother had not opened her eyes in two days. I whispered in her ear, "I support your decision to go, and I love you very much. You will be missed, but you need to be with your family." Feelings of delayed grief and anticipation of the unknown flooded my senses, so I walked out of the room to take a couple of breaths and stretch my legs. I heard Crackers the parrot chatting away, who lives in the rehabilitation room down the hall. He cheers up many people with his seemingly nonstop exciting chirps. He was "talking" so loudly about something. I felt like he called me, so I walked down the hallway to pet him as I often did. When I put my fingers in his cage, he bowed his head and gave me the top of his head to scratch. Sometimes it was hard to stop stroking him; I knew he needed human touch.

My mom loved birds. She talked about wanting parakeets since she was a child and told me repeatedly how birds were so smart. She knew this about all animals, and she loved Crackers too. I paused for a moment to take in the beauty and mystical wonder of his colors and his smooth, silky feathers. How simple and profound this moment of silence felt. Tension of the opposites: the worst possible pain of feeling helpless and anticipating my mom's passing. On the other side, a moment of experiencing the grace and power of a tiny bird, silencing the world for a moment. Refreshing yet haunting.

I felt an intuitive need to go back to Mom's room. I started the short walk down the longest corridor of my life. Life seemed to stand still as I walked toward her. When I got to her bed, she wasn't breathing. I realized it was at that exact moment when Crackers and I were connecting that my mother had taken her last breath. Crackers had called me to distract me so my mother could leave this physical earth without my being present.

Animals have always spoken to me, and to my mother, so it makes sense that today I am a professional animal communicator. While mourning the loss of my greatest gift and teacher, I discovered another gift: the ability to telepathically connect with animals.

Doris Carol Perrault left the physical world on May 15, 2023, one day after Mother's Day and one week after she and I "felt" her decision to transition. She did it her way, on her own terms, always according to her timeline.

Realizing her departure, a lump formed in my throat, a knot in my stomach clenched, and my nervous system became immobilized by the excruciating pain of loss and sorrow. I felt numbness and pins and needles overtaking my whole body. I knew I would remember this moment forever.

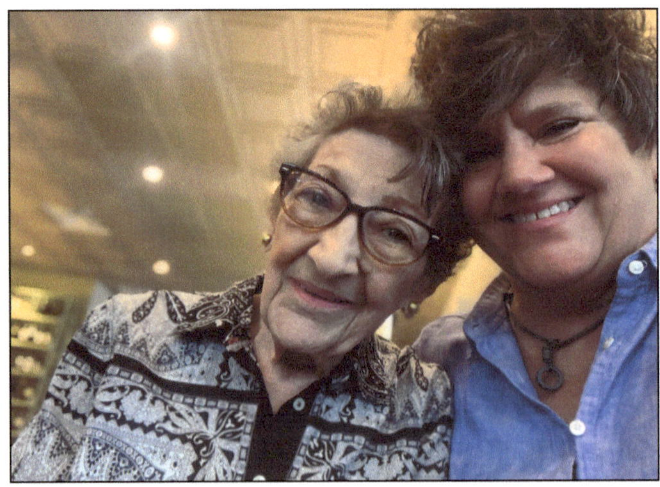

About This Book

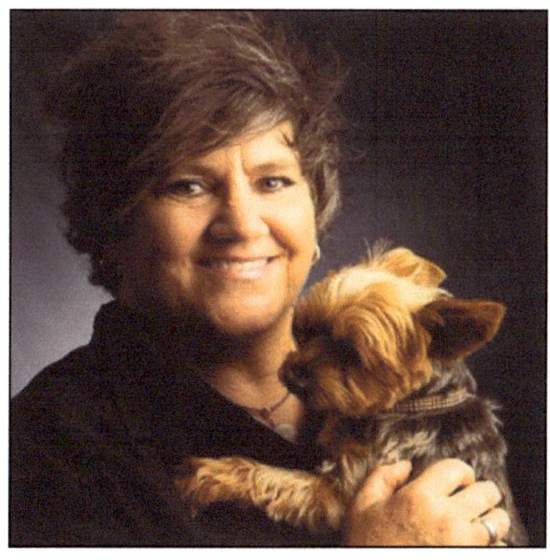

My mother's dementia stripped away years of doubt, fear, and regret in her and opened up her deepest self: pure consciousness. It was like I was looking straight through to her heart light: who she came into this world as. The glow and love that emanated from her were contagious. This remarkable sight inspired me to visually represent what I was feeling and seeing. Painting has always been a way for me to process emotions. As passionately as my mother supported me as an artist, I felt equally as passionate to pick up my paintbrush and begin painting souls. Almost effortlessly, I painted a masterpiece: a visual representation, an emotional and energetic imprint, of my mother's and my soul together titled *Mom and Me.*

My mother taught me how to trust myself, and for that I'm forever grateful. Through these paintings, I turned my confusion and loss into new life. My art represents that new life; its meaning is chosen by the viewer, the observer. When I paint the soul of a person or animal, I attempt to turn tragedy into possibility, despair into renewal and wonder. My mother inspired me to create an art form that speaks a new language.

Colors of Consciousness is a combination of the metaphysical world and the art world. Each spread is laid out with the human or animal communication in words and a beautifully composed painting of that being's soul or consciousness.

Energy and consciousness inhabit a physical form. Each soul's energy is translated into dynamic color and descriptive mark-making on the canvas surface. Each sentient being is different, and so is the soul and energy that flows through it.

Animals, like humans, are sentient beings with consciousness. They have free will, are intelligent, and experience emotions, thoughts, likes, dislikes, and feelings. All humans and animals come into this world nonverbal, relying on their senses to communicate. As humans grow, we slowly build a vocabulary. As words dominate and take over as a means of communication, the nonverbal falls away, leaving our telepathic connections dormant. Perhaps this explains why we have such a deep connection with our animal friends for love and companionship. We subconsciously remember when we used to communicate telepathically and intuitively.

Each soul, essence, consciousness, or being (whatever name you give it) has identifying and resonating colors. The way the colors and designs come together is as miraculous and personal as one's thumb or paw print and as unique as one's voice, eye color, and laugh. This book will explore all of these captivating aesthetics and more. An abstract world of painting souls has indeed been born, revealing itself through each sentient being I paint and communicate with.

This book is literally a work of art in progress. My passion is intuiting the energy in humans and animals and revealing their soul expression on the canvas. My hope is that every soul will see and feel what I do when I paint them. This energy of love and light that each painting illuminates changes our perceptions and inspires love, growth, and discovery.

What if we were to contemplate and appreciate the inner beauty in everyone we encountered as colors, light, or a unique design, like a well-developed abstract painting, rather than by outside appearances, such as skin tone, body shape, or even race? How might this change the way we relate and create? How different life could be if we acknowledged and honored

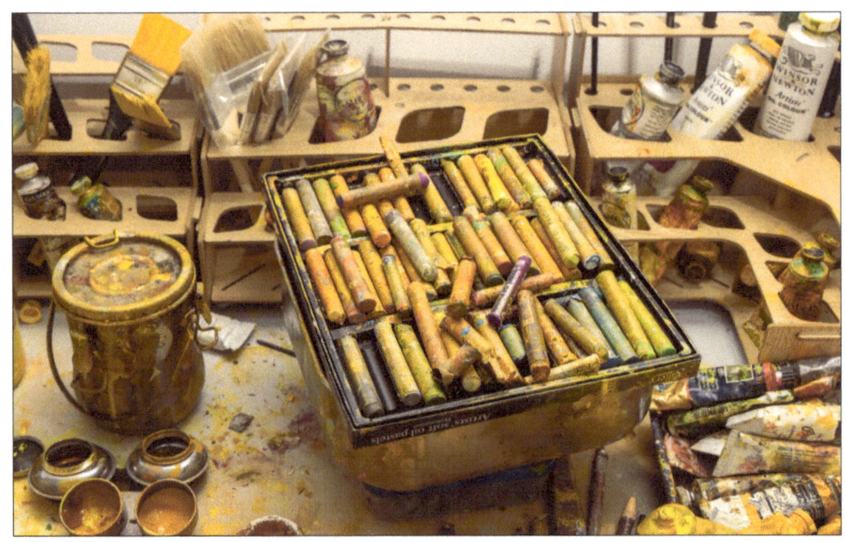

the beauty in every soul. How freeing might it be to let go of judgment and instead practice acceptance and compassion as we celebrate our differences.

Painting souls allows me as an artist to reach people individually and collectively at the same time. Shapes, colors, lines, and textures speak for themselves without unnecessary noise, commentary, or unwanted opinion. Sometimes people are unaware they are healing wounded parts of themselves as they pause to take in the transformational energy of a soul painting. Elements such as color or shape in the artwork may remind them of moments in their past or validate a deep and perhaps hidden emotion.

By feeling with our gut and not thinking with our head, we are able to create a safe space for contemplation and growth. This momentary suspension in thought may serve as a grounding or launch of sorts that leads to healing parts of ourselves. Through this cathartic exchange of viewer and soul energy related to viewing the soul painting itself, we are reminded of our true self or essence.

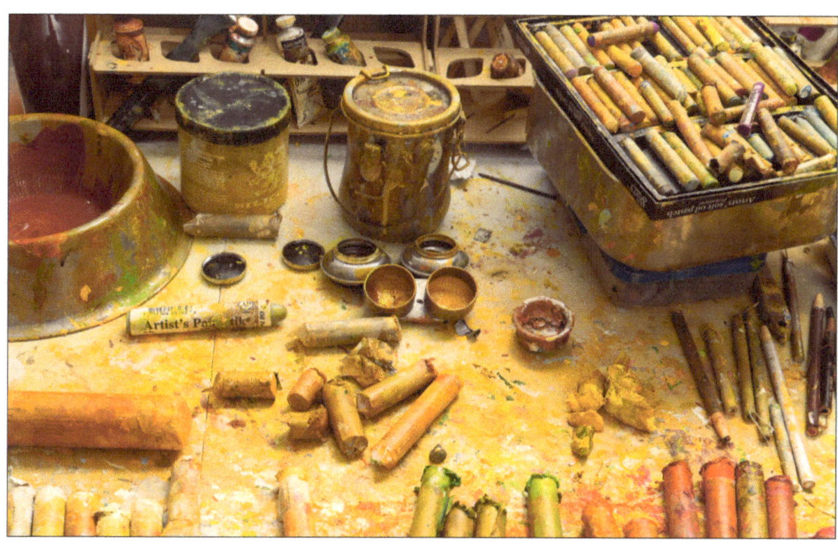

Why Abstract Art?

Art changes people by its mere presence. The energy of art changes the energy in the room it inhabits. It expands our hearts and minds and opens us to new possibilities. Being open to new experiences changes the frequency of sounds and energy all around us. Art adds to this dynamic energy that is constantly evolving and changing. Art infuses a beautiful essence or expansion of love and light into our shared collective consciousness. Eric Kandel, Nobel Prize-winning neuropsychiatrist in *Reductionism in Art and Brain Science,* states, "Great art is great because it's ambiguous."[1] Great abstract art has that ambiguity. It brings the viewer to attentiveness so they can bring more of themselves to a work of art to complete the story or the emotion. Kandel also stated, "Our neural circuitry is hardwired to prefer images we can identify, which makes abstract forms more difficult to process. At the same time, abstract forms leave the door open to interpretation, stimulating the higher-level areas of the brain responsible for creativity and imagination."[2]

Looking at abstract art on a regular basis can actually make you more creative and intelligent as you fire off new neurons. Kandel notes in his book that "abstract art provides a stimuli to our visual system that violates almost all of the rules that the visual system evolved to look for and process. As a result, our bottom-up system of processing looks for lines, figures, perspective, etc. to complete the story."[3]

Art changes according to the state of mind of the viewer, especially abstract art. What you see in the painting one day you might not see the next, and so it goes. It is like having a new work of art to view each time you interact with it; a new adventure and story to complete. The definition of *miracle* I am drawn to most is "a change in perception." Since abstract art invites you, the viewer, to be the seer and to perceive, you indeed must be a miracle.

About the Poems

The poems that juxtapose each painting are words, feelings, and knowing I receive from Spirit while completing each painting. The poems are unique gifts each soul brings with them to this physical form. They are what Spirit wants each soul to know about themselves for healing and love.

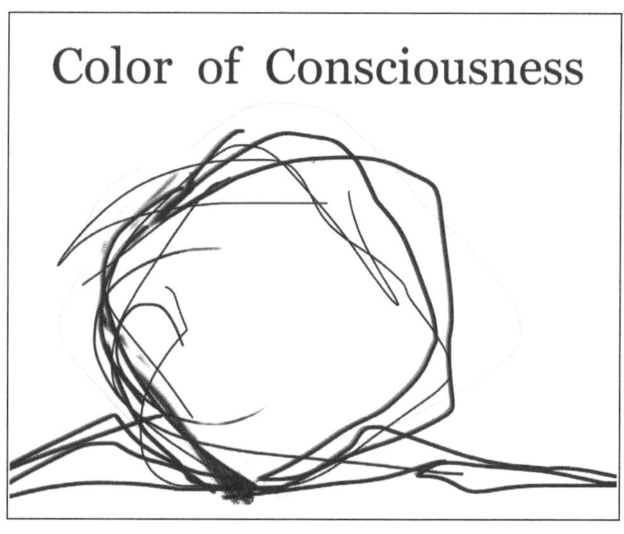

SOUL PAINTINGS

VAN AND AMY

Meant to Be
20" x 20" oil on board

Hello, Dear Soul,

Deep inside
without words is a knowing.
I will love you

to the end of time,
beyond our hearts and minds.

Into the heavens
in the spaciousness of love,

you will remind me how it feels.

How our love reveals
all parts of ourselves.

Thank you for these many gifts.

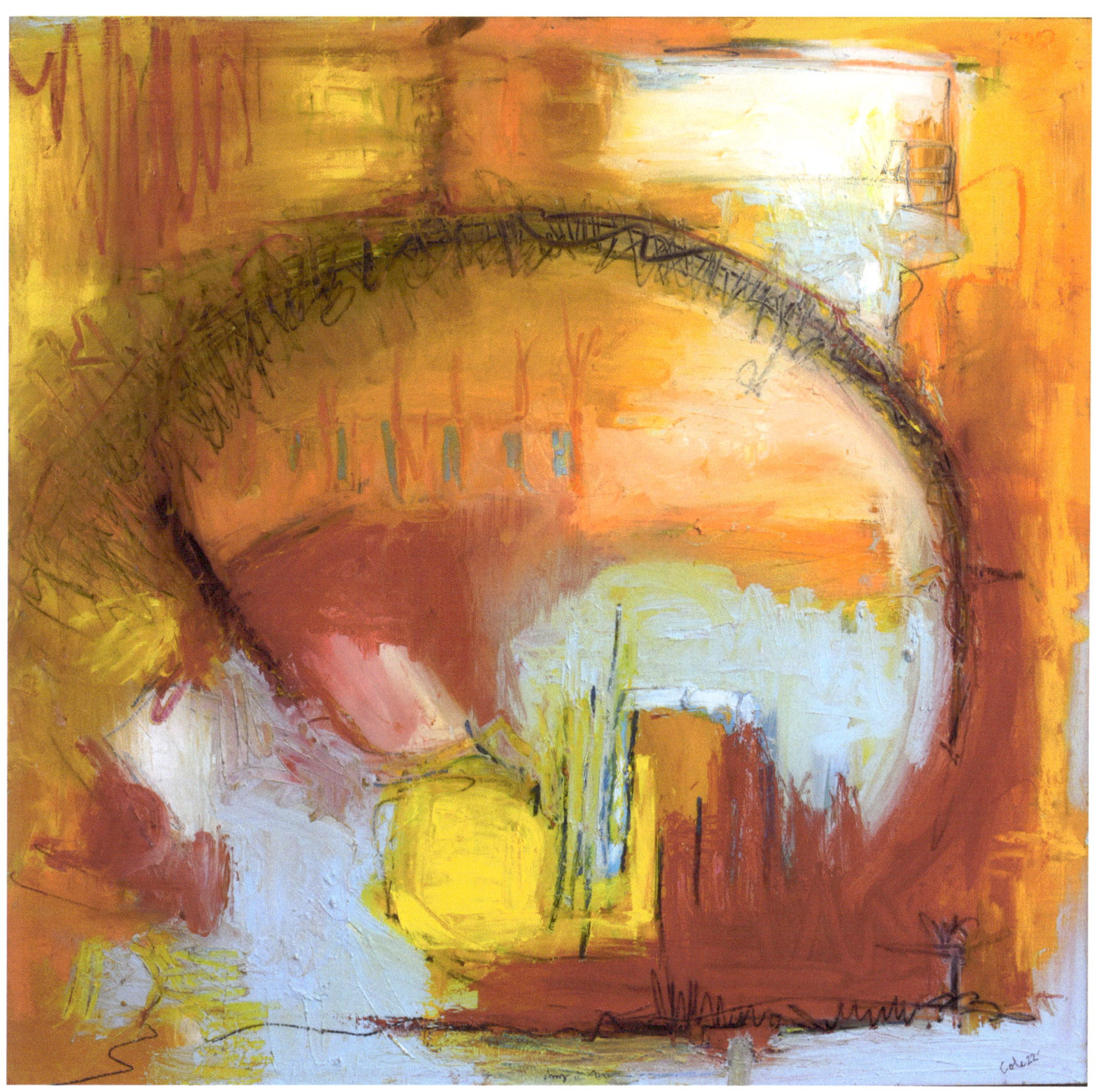

DORIS AND NICOLE

Mother and Daughter
20" x 20" oil on board

Hello, Dear Soul,

Together again
in the world of the living,

intermeshing our thoughts
of joy and laughter,

allowing love to fill our hearts
and spill over into one another.

Surrounded by love, we say goodnight.

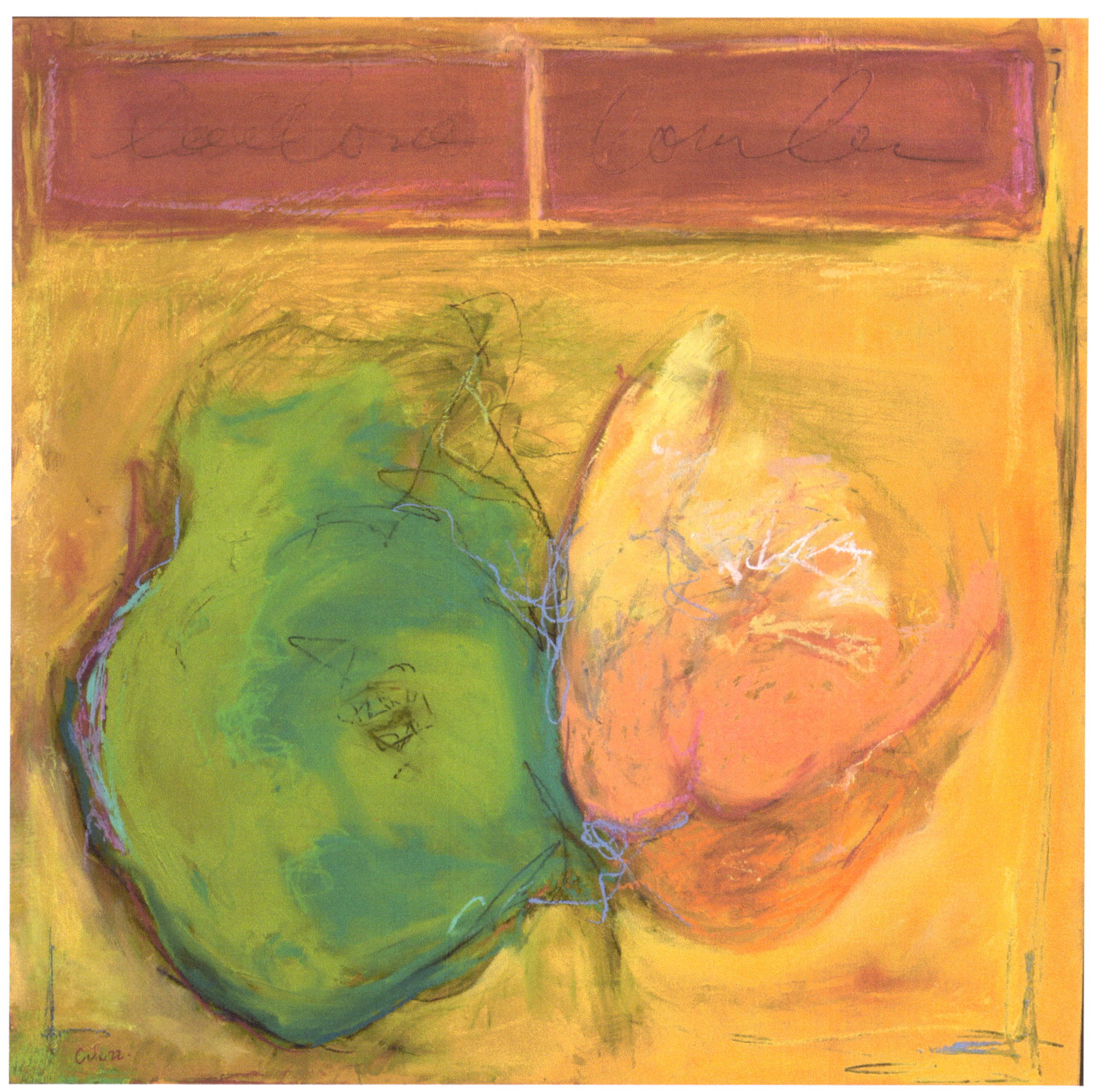

STEPHANIE (client and her guide)

Wren
20" x 20" oil on board

Hello, Dear Soul and Guide,

You come to life,
written in the stars.

Me in front, you behind.

We dive and dip in sync, face-to-face,
splashing about. Yellows, browns, gold allures.

Invite the joy we possess,

the animals of destiny by our side.
Within our hearts, freedom is here.

Love, in our hands, is waiting to be named.

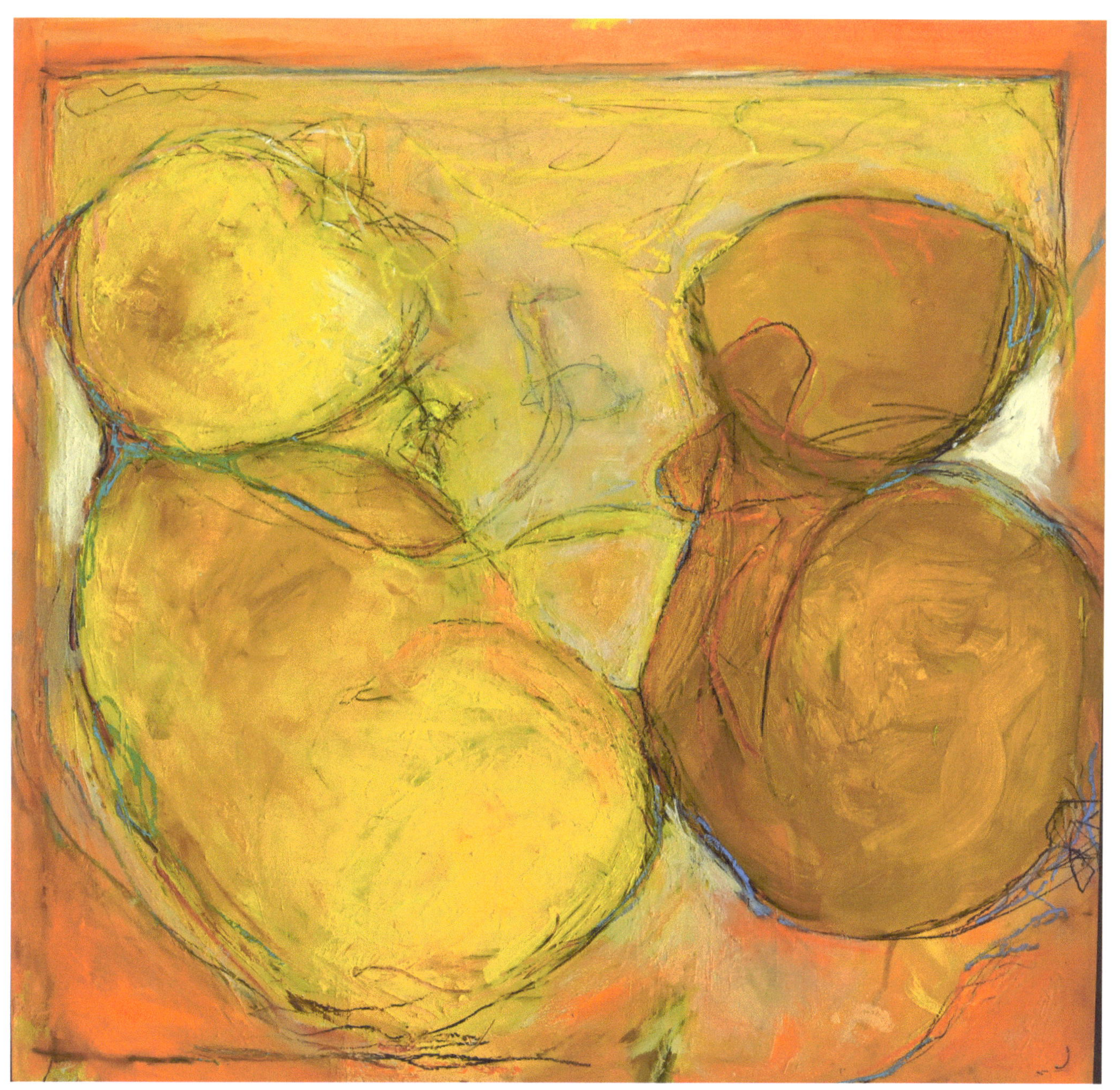

AUSTIN
Bright-Eyed and Bushy-Tailed
20" x 20" oil on board

Hello, Dear Soul,

You are wide open to the world
and its mysteries.
We are thankful for your presence.

With gratitude,
we admire your ability to meet us
at our soul's level.

Excited about all things new,
to frolic with playful adieu,
bouncing back and forth in contentment,

renewed for another day.

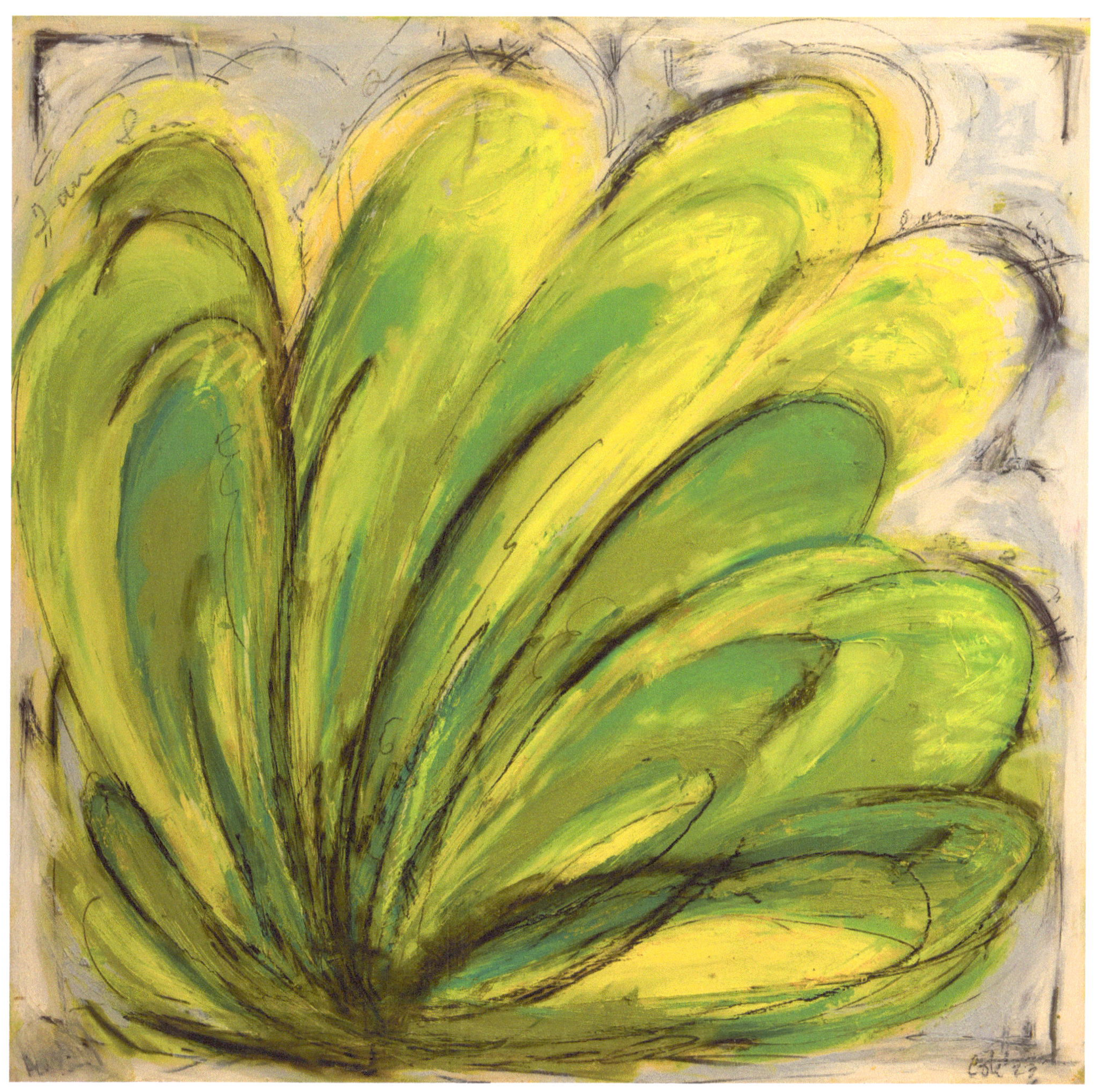

KENSLEE

Komorebi (Koh-mo-reh-bee)
20" x 20" oil on board

Hello, Dear Soul,

You filter in and out
of the tree canopy.

Highlighted by the dappled
lighting that filters your shy
yet confident glow.

Young soul, you smile
of journeys experienced

with a vision of what is yet to come.
Your effortless beauty and imagination
propels you across the ground,

aimed toward the innocence
of your kindness and the unknown.

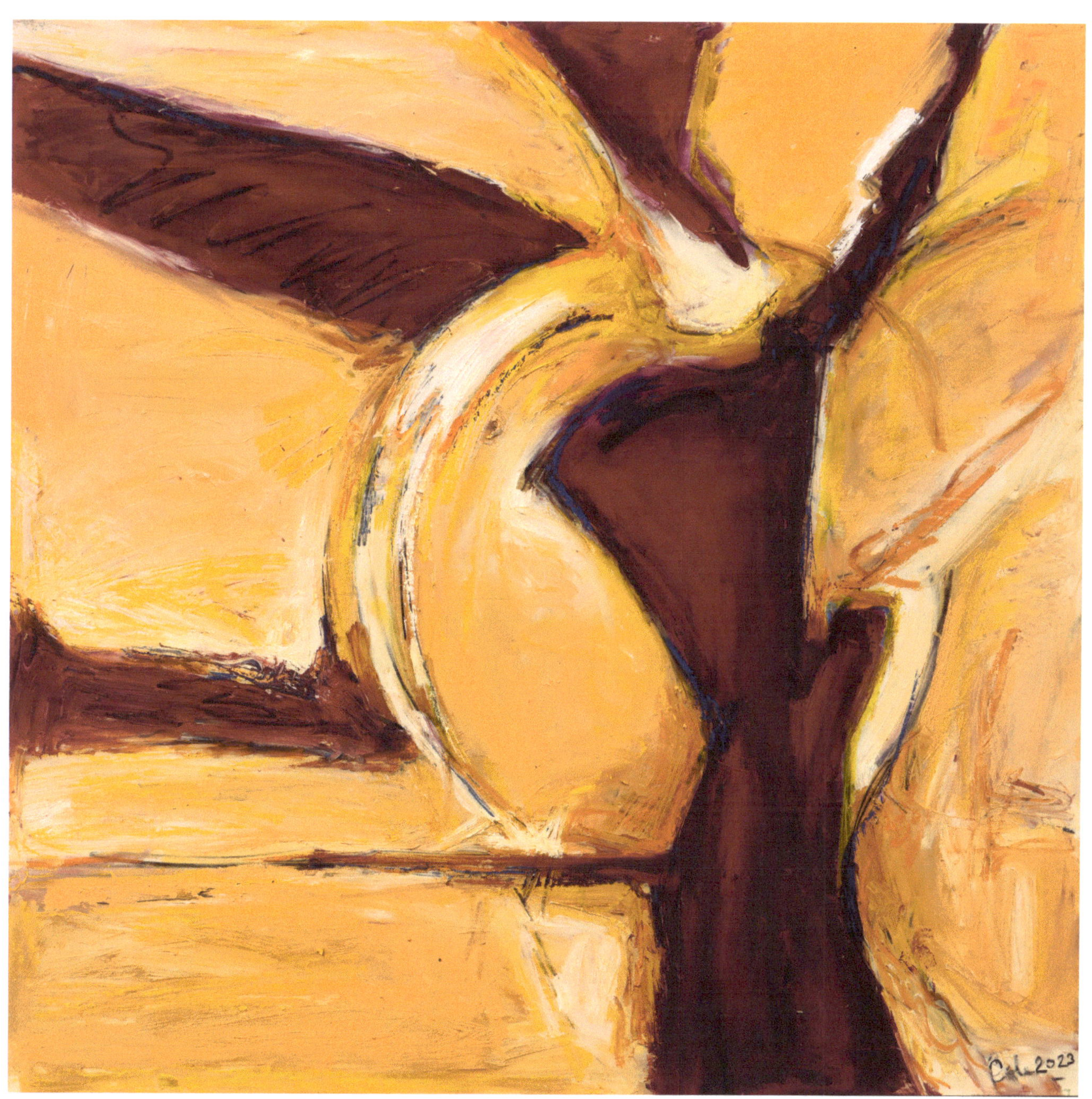

ANGELA

Vast Layers
20" x 20" oil on board

Hello, Dear Soul,

The depth of your insight
is prosperous,
mentally and spiritually.
You see through to the core.

You thrive
in nature, in the morning
and evening.
Sublime sounds crackle

in the golden hour, driven
into rest, with divine

love for family.

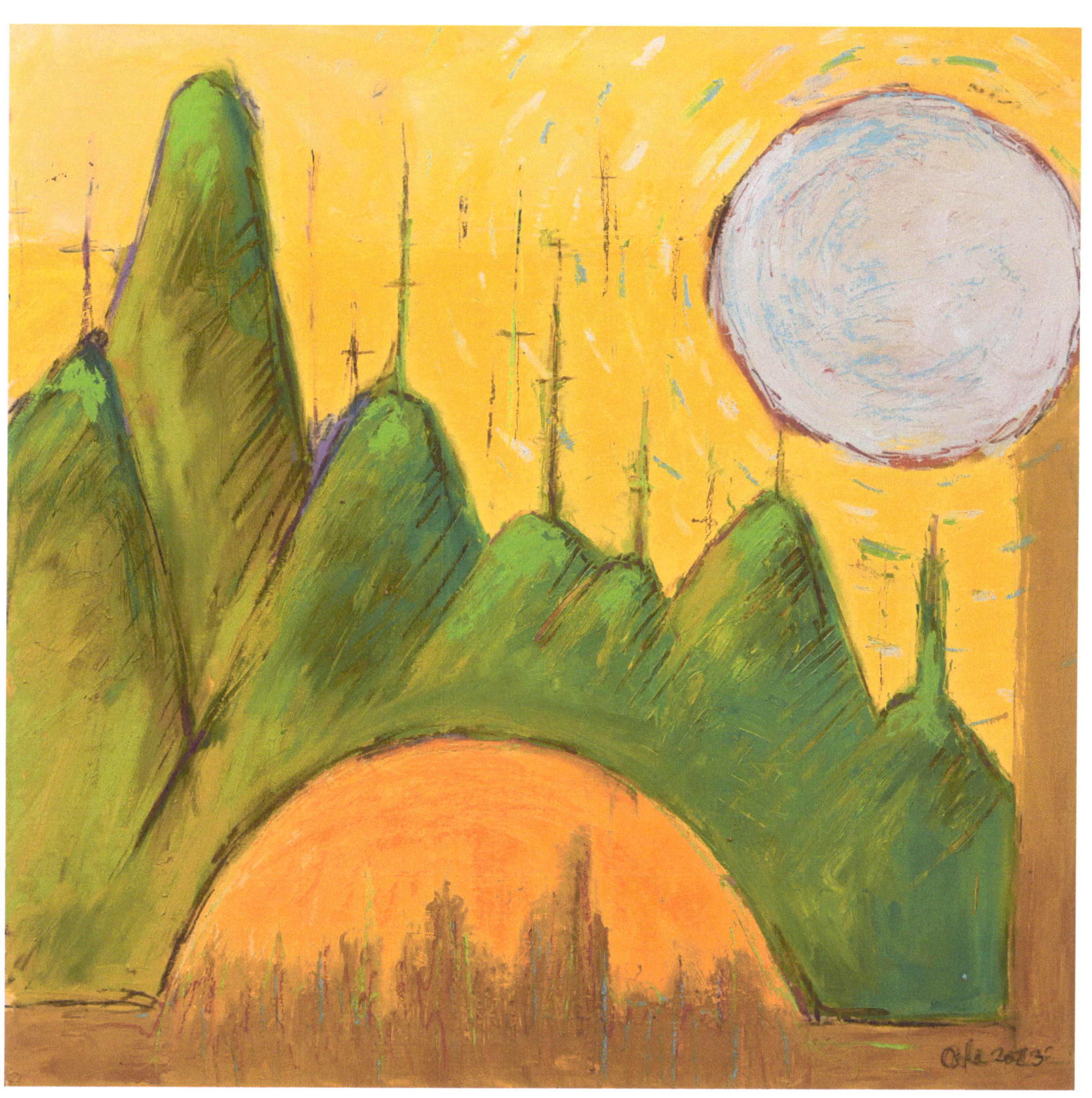

PAULA AND MARIA

You Push, I Pull
20" x 20" oil on board

Hello, Dear Souls,

A tunnel, weaving through oxygen
and molecules, your beings
intertwine, up and up.

In the vortex, you become one.
Threads of color support the whole;
you twist and whine.

To exist and breathe between night and day,
bowing down with grace
at the meeting of one another.

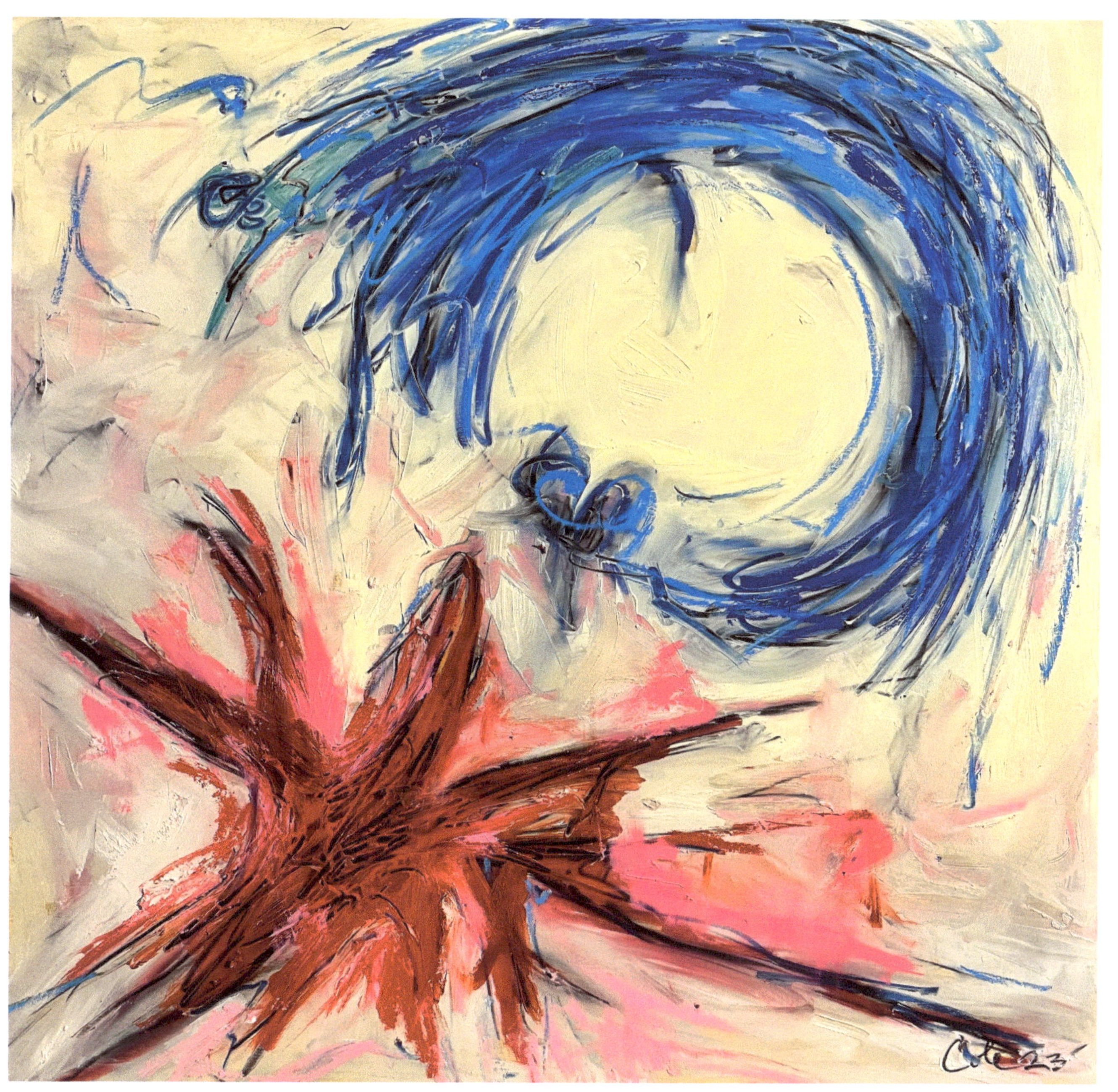

KATHY

This Way Is Up
36" x 48" oil on canvas

Hello, Dear Soul,

See yourself, your inner glory
steeped in childhood play
and earth energy.

Open to the vastness of Mother Earth.
Glow and move.
Live in the golden light of love forever.

Spread your magnificent intent,
wide overhead, crossing many distances,
seen and heard.

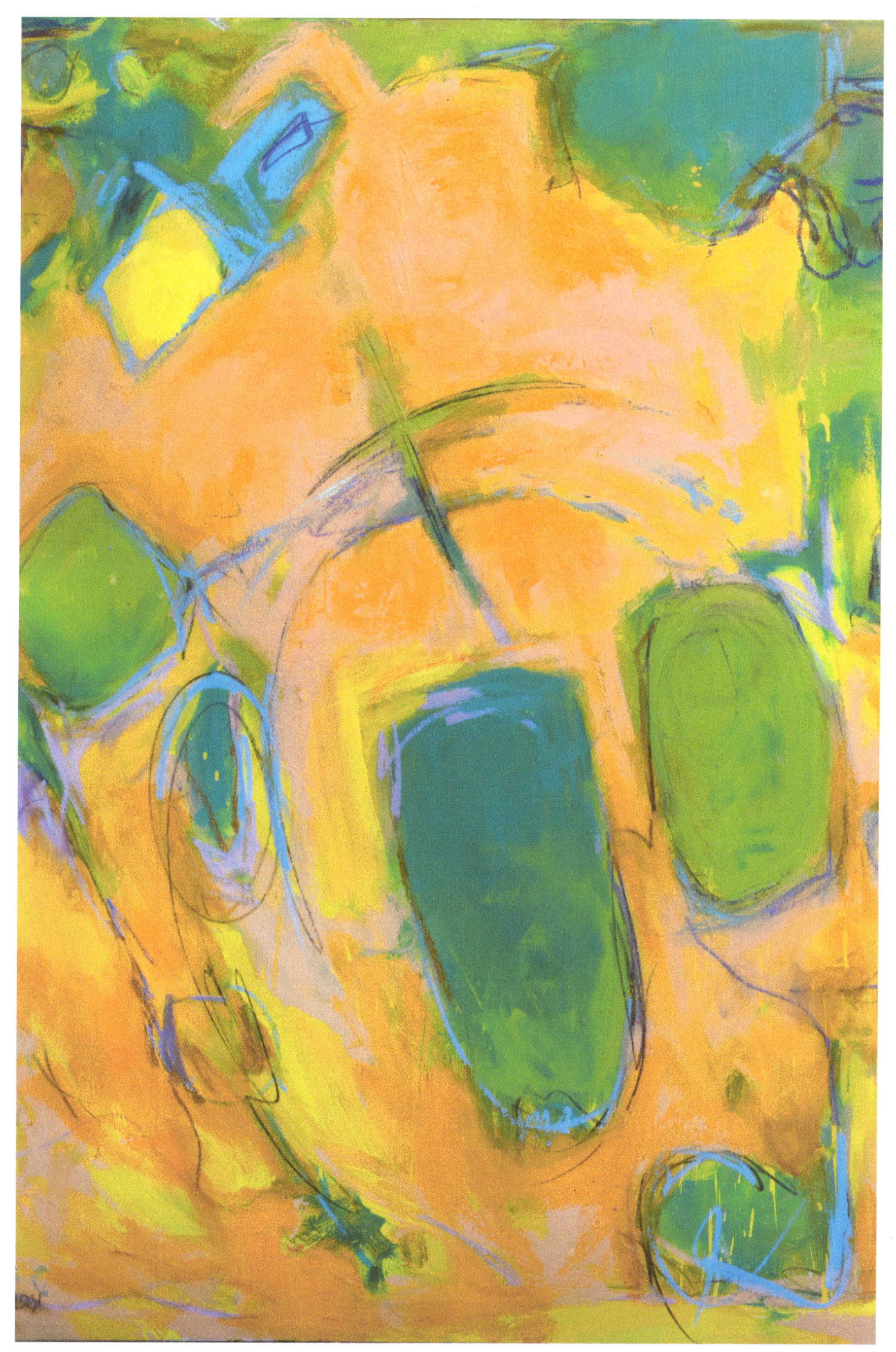

PUPPIES

Puppy Collective #1
36" x 48" oil on canvas

At birth your mission is so vulnerable,
giving of love and accepting.

You are raw, pure happiness.

In the next incarnation,
may you fulfill your soul's journey.

This painting is for all young puppy souls
who never made it to adulthood.

We love you to the moon and back,
from the soul of souls to the highest point.

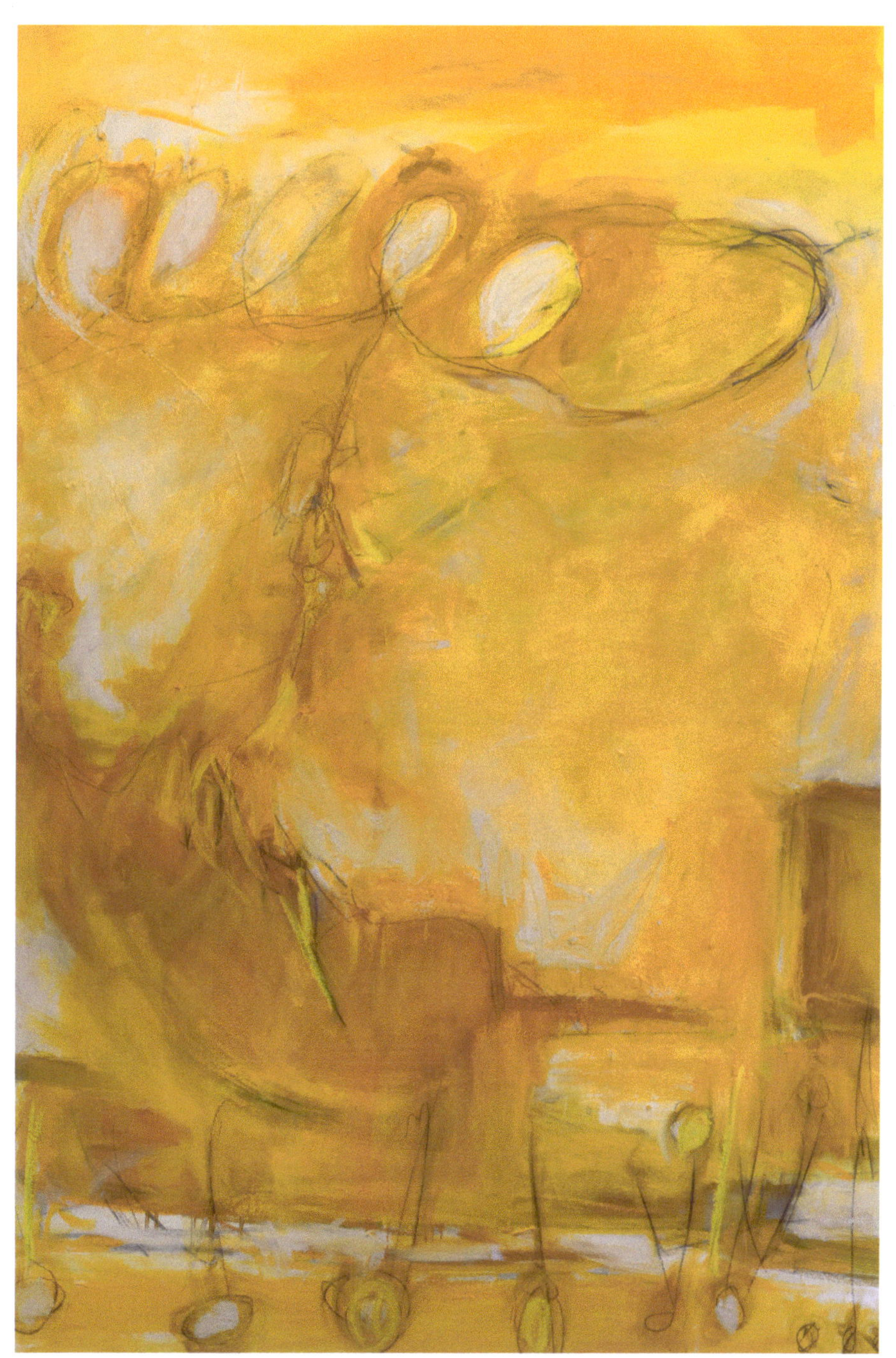

RABBITS

Jiggly Boo I
36" x 48" oil on canvas

Hello, Dear Soul,

Your voices are quiet, yet many.
Around every corner,
curiosity and lack of safety awaits you.

Your unwavering commitment to bounce about,
makes me shake with happiness and laughter.

You are heaven forever, inside and out.
You embody peace and strength.

You own your vulnerability.

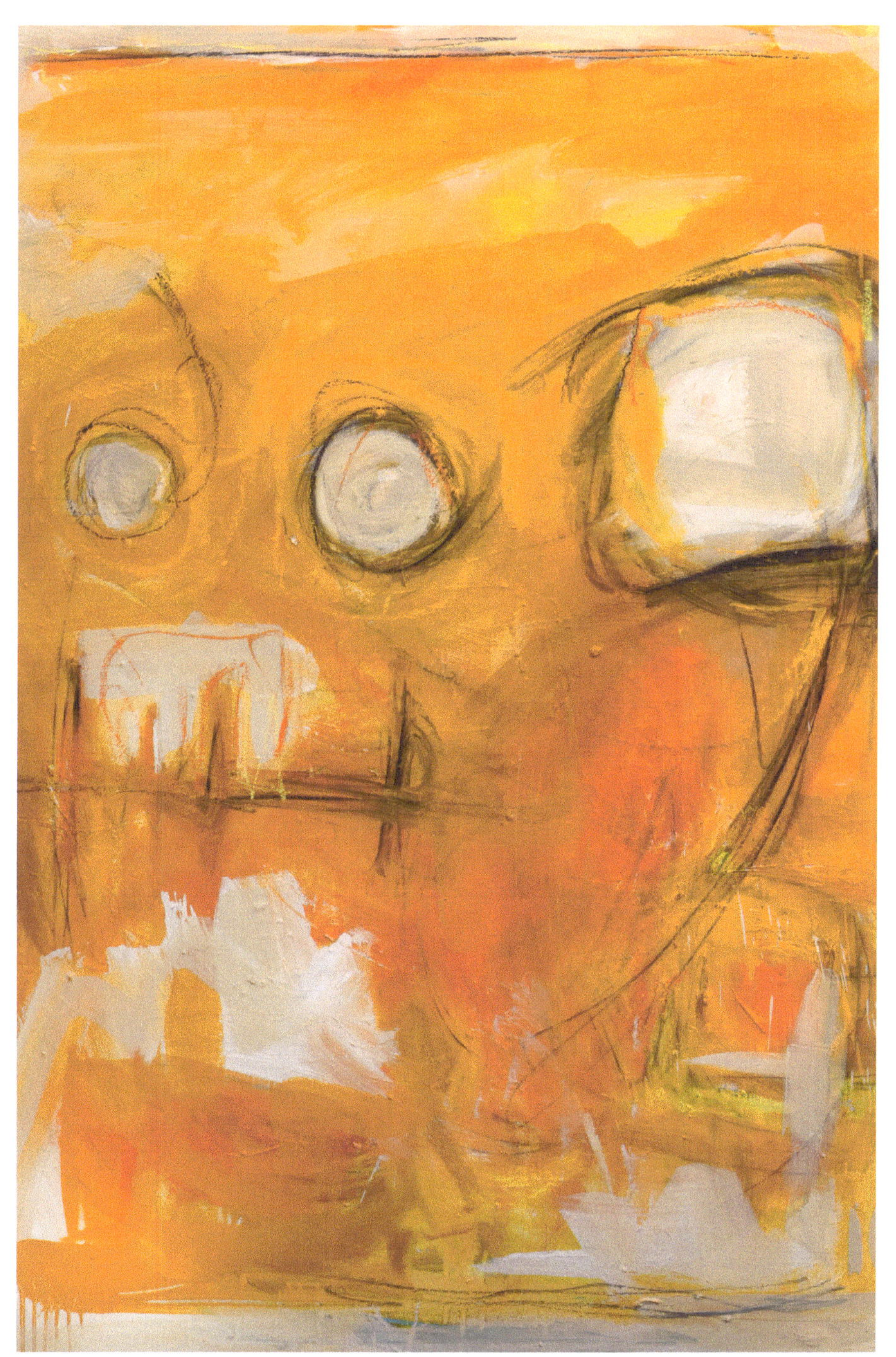

HORSES

Wild Horses I
40" x 60" oil on canvas

Hello, Dear Soul,

They call you by name,
but you don't come. Why would you?

Free, unbound, your feet rhythmically
round the ground, again and again,
until you are out of breath.

Exhilarating and honest,
your presence is liberating.
I am in AWE of your depth.

May we learn from your earnest ways.

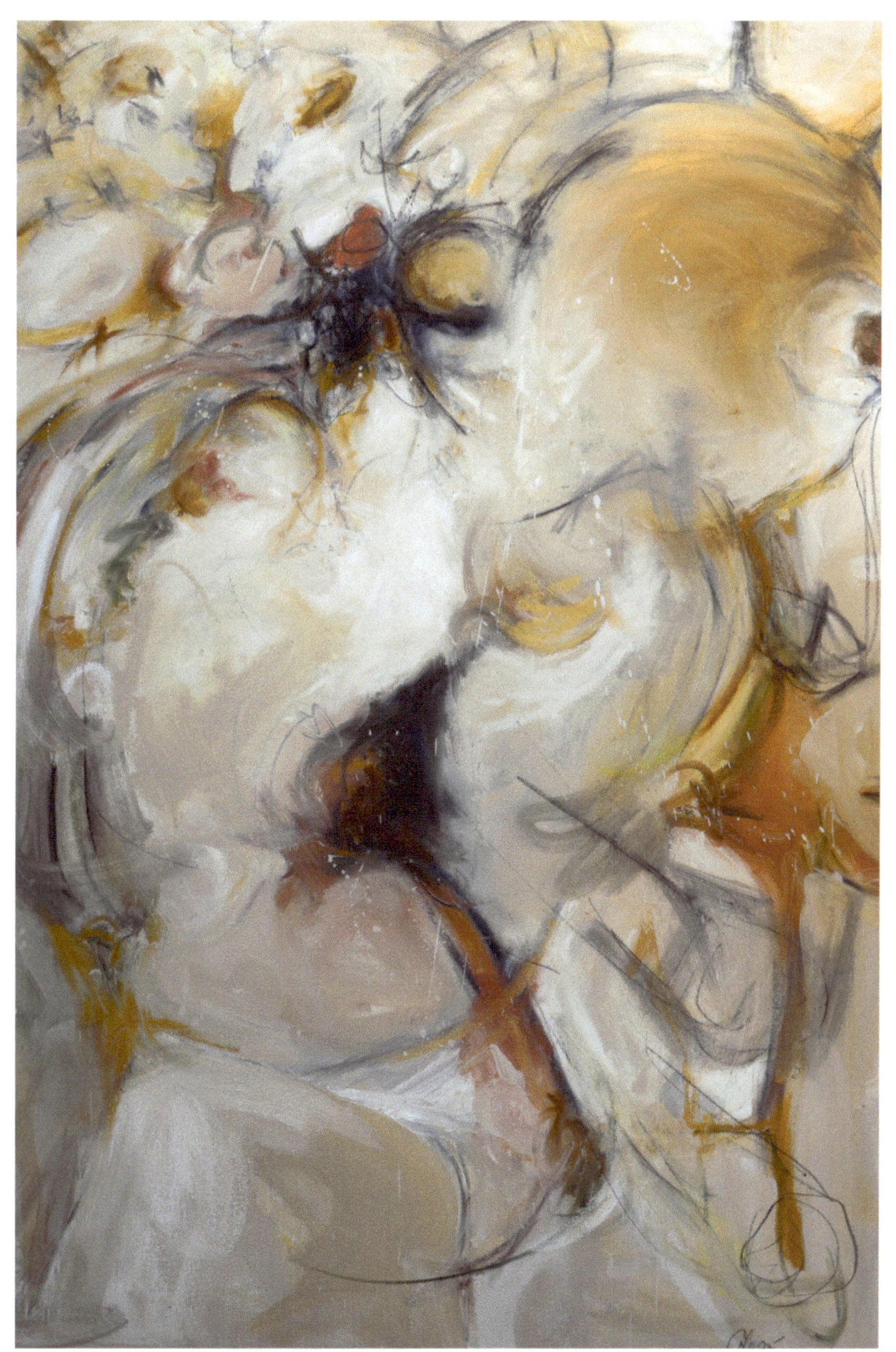

MOTHERS AND DAUGHTERS

Peripheral I and II
(2) 36" x 48" oil on canvas

Hello, Dear Souls,

I hear the voices of mothers
and daughters who have come before
in your divine wisdom to learn and teach.

To create and be created, we divide and conquer.
Let us paint our experience with a wide brush
of color and exuberance until the day is done.

Through our eyes, live the colors of love.

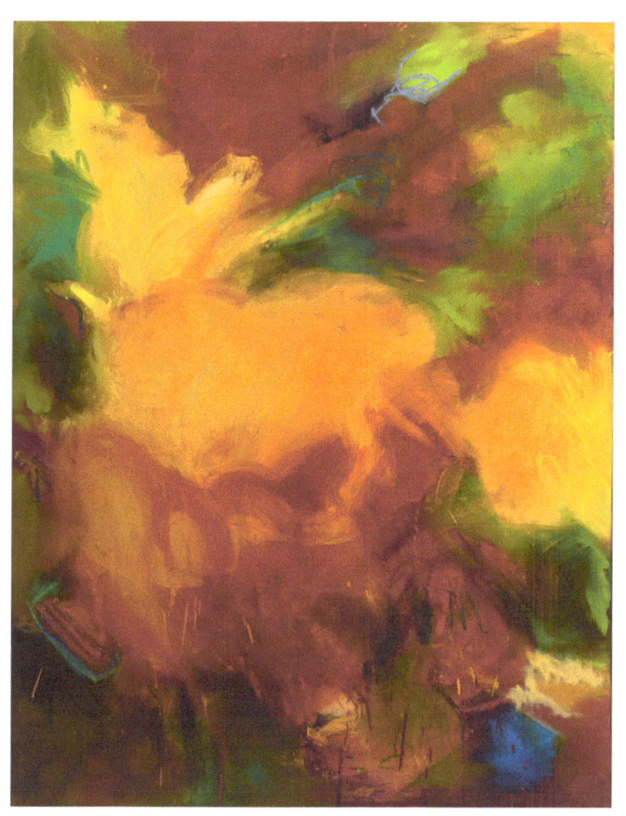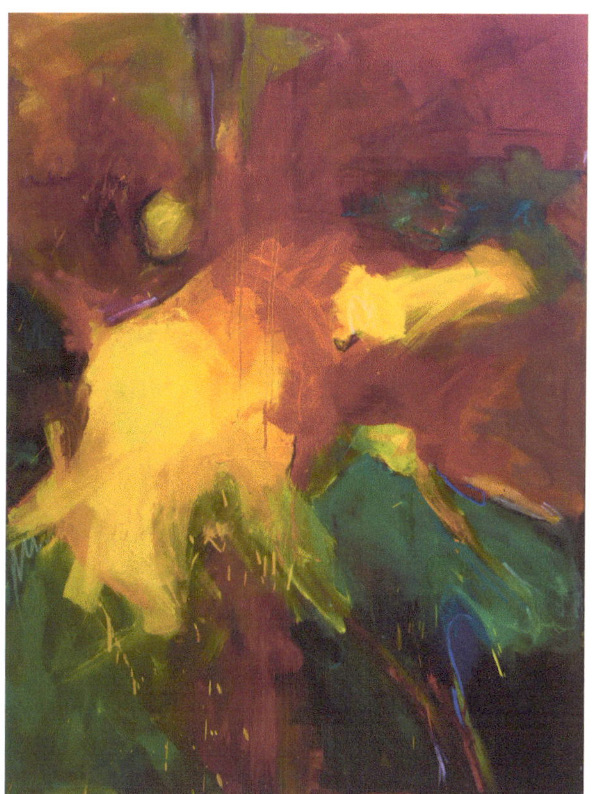

AMY

All Is Aglow
40" x 60" oil on canvas

Hello, Dear Soul,

Rise to your feet, swinging
strength of force and power.

Leaning into the foreground,
you gather momentum,
making your mark on poetry and love.

Channeling strength and glorious
power, you rise above, recharging
in your silence..

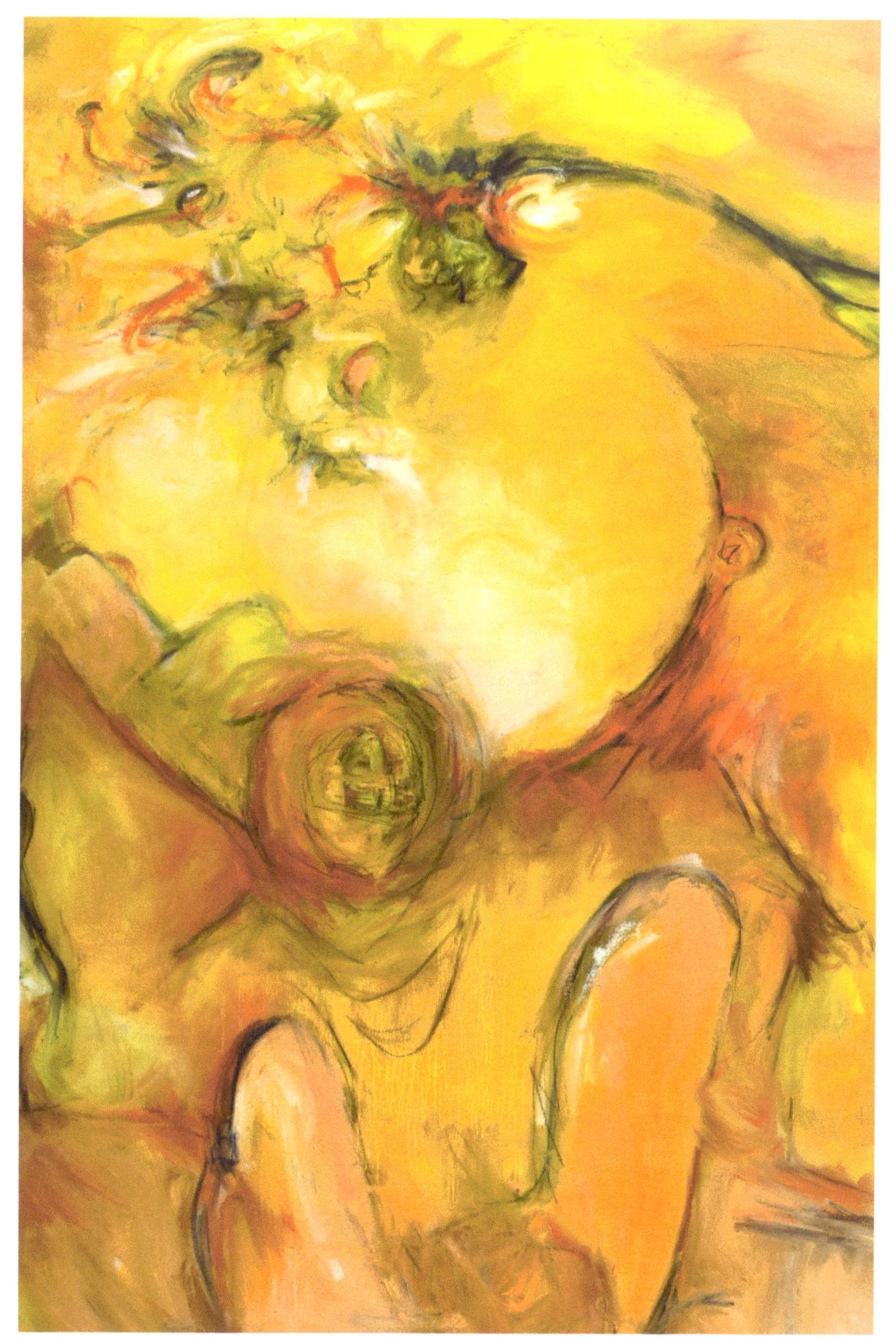

AZULAH

Inside of Love
20" x 20" oil on board

Hello, Dear Soul,

You speak and spell with excitement.
We know it's not the end,
so it must be the beautiful beginning.

Let us in; we rejoice to sing your praises
with harmony and hope
in the soft delicacies of your voice and smile.

We bow and pray for the universe
to bring us more of you;
we realize when our prayers are answered.

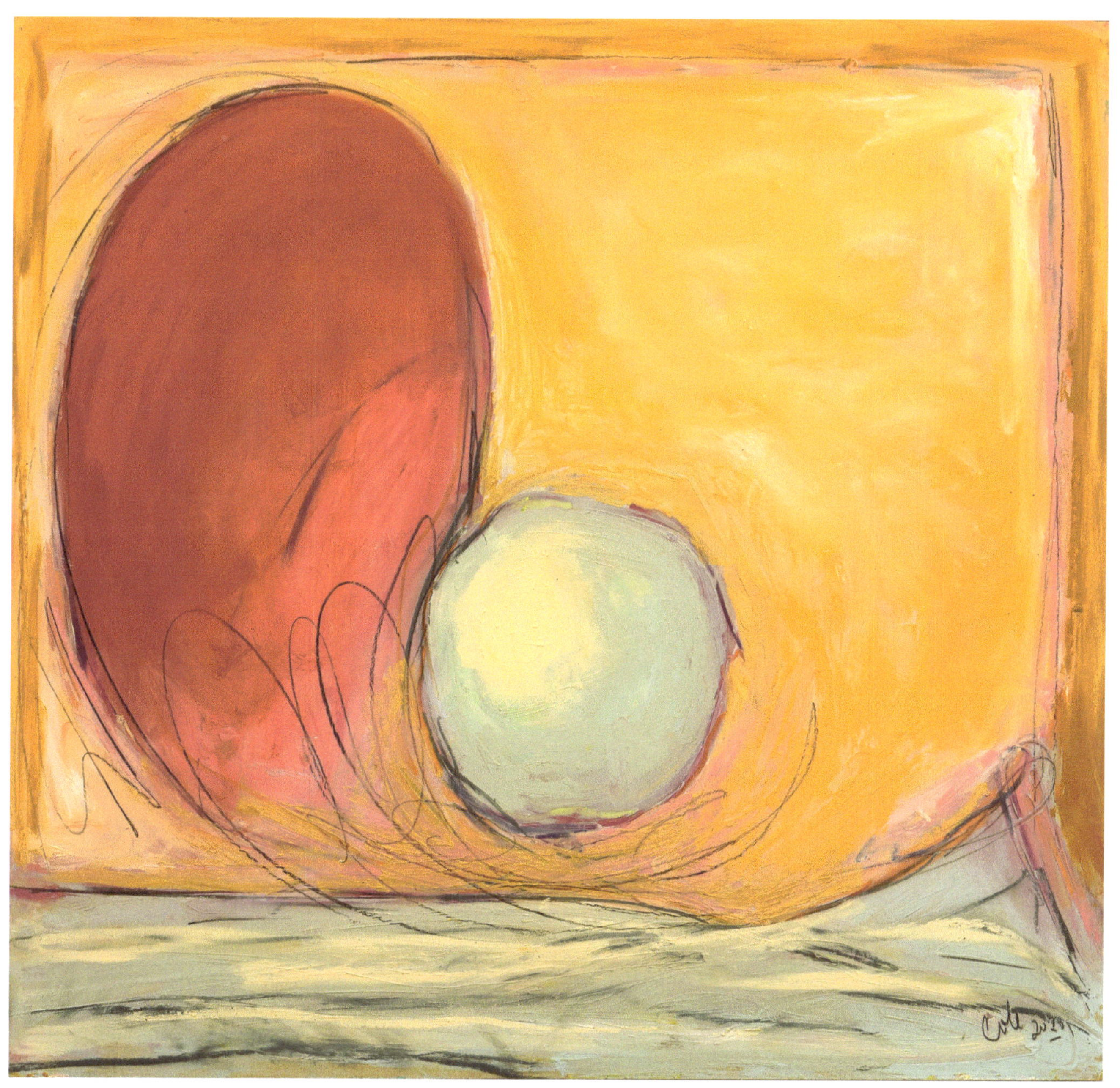

BABY CAKES (feline)

Slick
20" x 20" oil on board

Hello, Dear Soul,

You write the rules
we live by. Days of thrills,

highs and never lows,
you allow us to be.

Your soul is God-like
with the reverence of bright light.

Thank you for accepting this
world of false promises

by flipping it upside down.

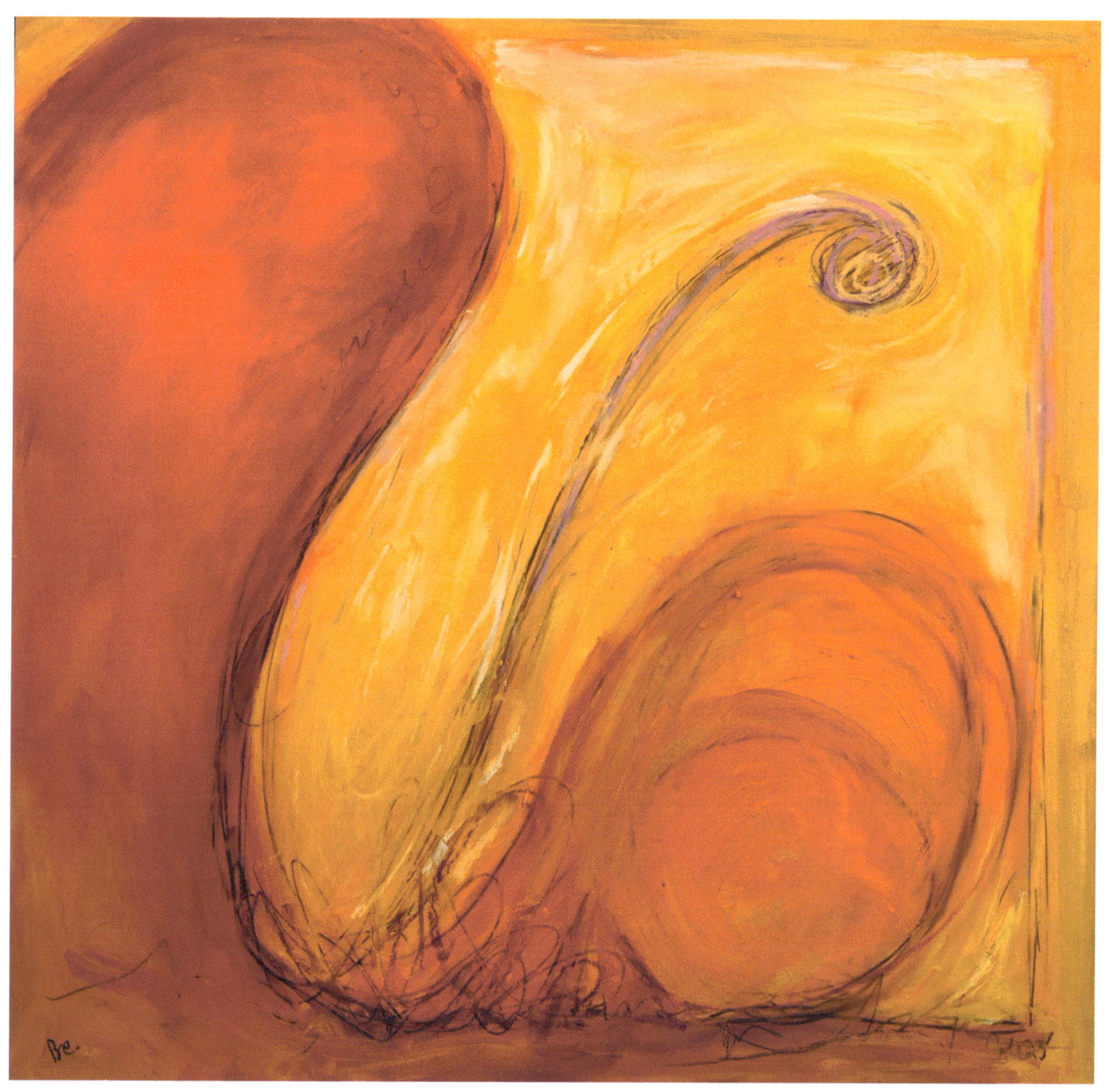

LUCY

"Lucy Lu" (dog)
20" x 20" oil on board

Hello, Dear Soul,

A cross between heaven and earth.
That's where I arrived.

When I first met you,
with excitement we did thrive.

Decorated with beauty
as our lives spin and weave.

Sonic speed ahead, you scream.
Riding the rails, waiting to exhale.

Taking the corner more carefully now.
No need to risk it all.

Heaven is my earth, until my rebirth.

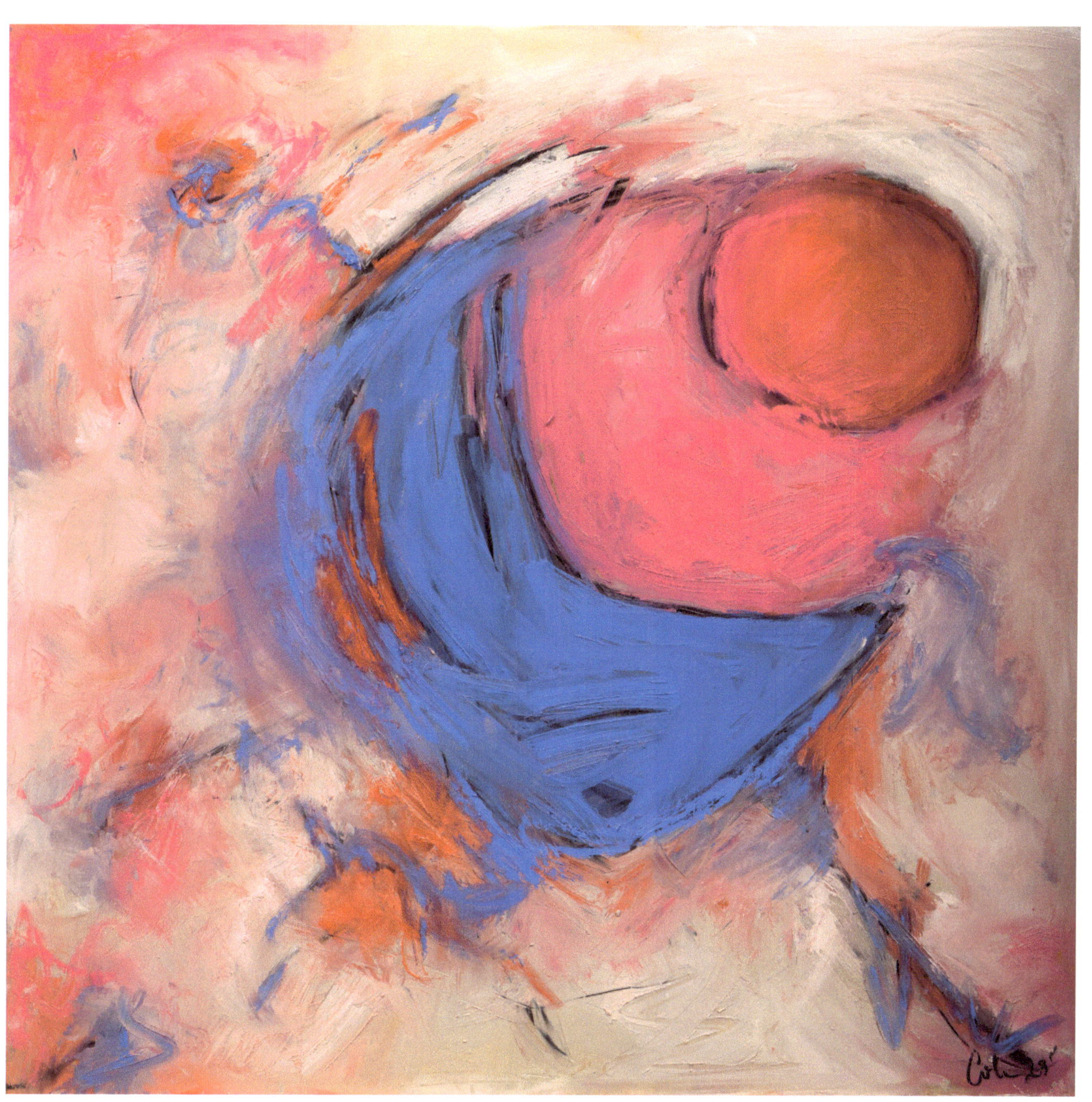

SUZI

The Sea's Balance
20" x 20" oil on board

Hello, Dear Soul,
One way or another, your name is known.
Calling on the sea to strengthen Earth's vibrations.

We feel your waves of energy,
longing to recharge.

Diving, dipping, swimming through barricades
of existence, clinging to the love that got you here.

One of the strongest, your might is sure,
unaware of power you endure

Open and free, you belong to sea. Your gift is simple,
carpenter bee.

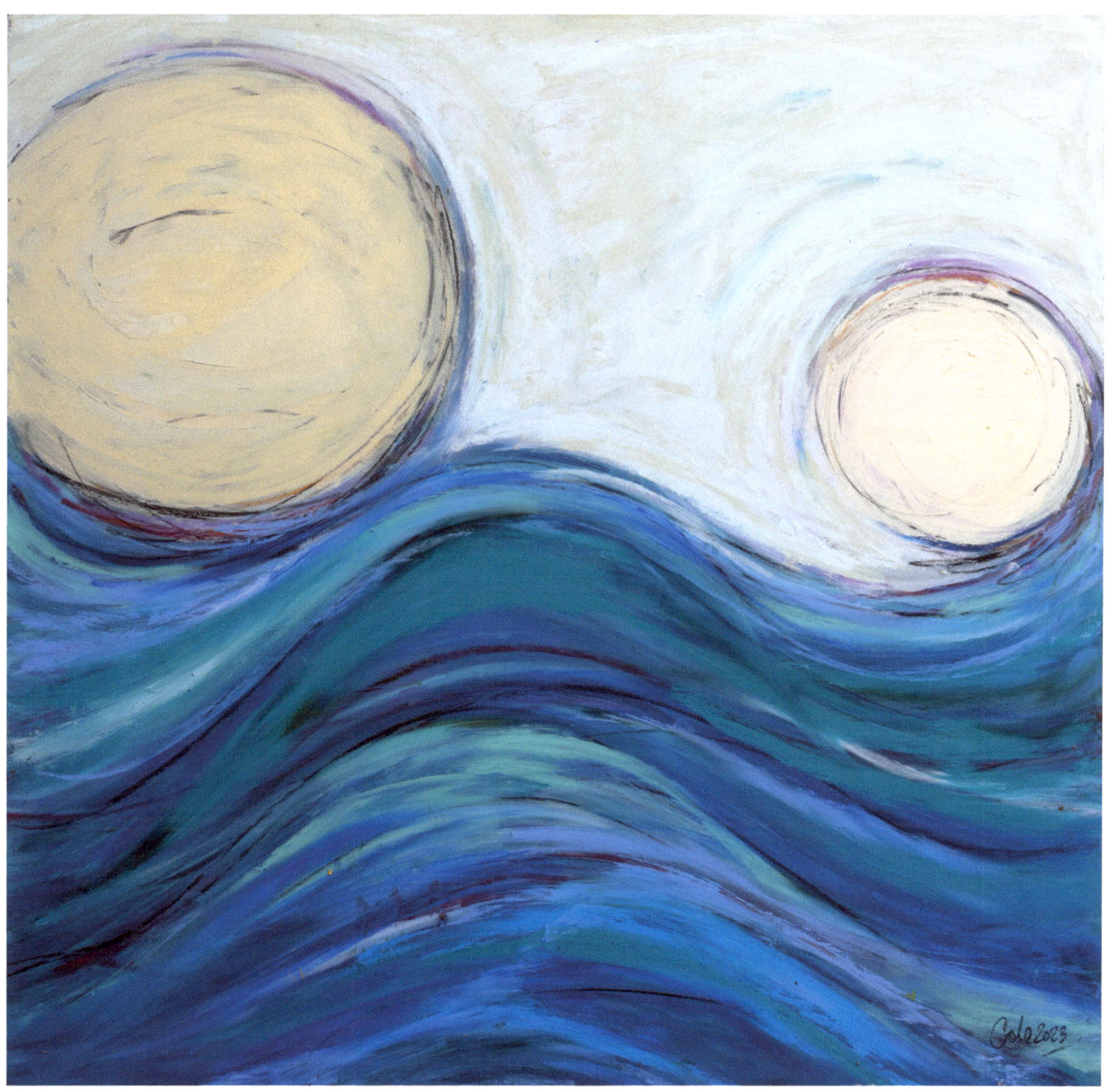

51 · Colors of Consciousness

CHARLIE (canine)

Char-Char Chaboggie
20" x 20" oil on board

Hello, Dear Soul,

Your glorious light illuminates all
that is good in this world.

All is love; all is companionship.
Your earthy significance, magic,

bursting in all directions, captivating
our hearts. "Be soft, be gentle,"

you remind us to be,
in every way with gratitude.

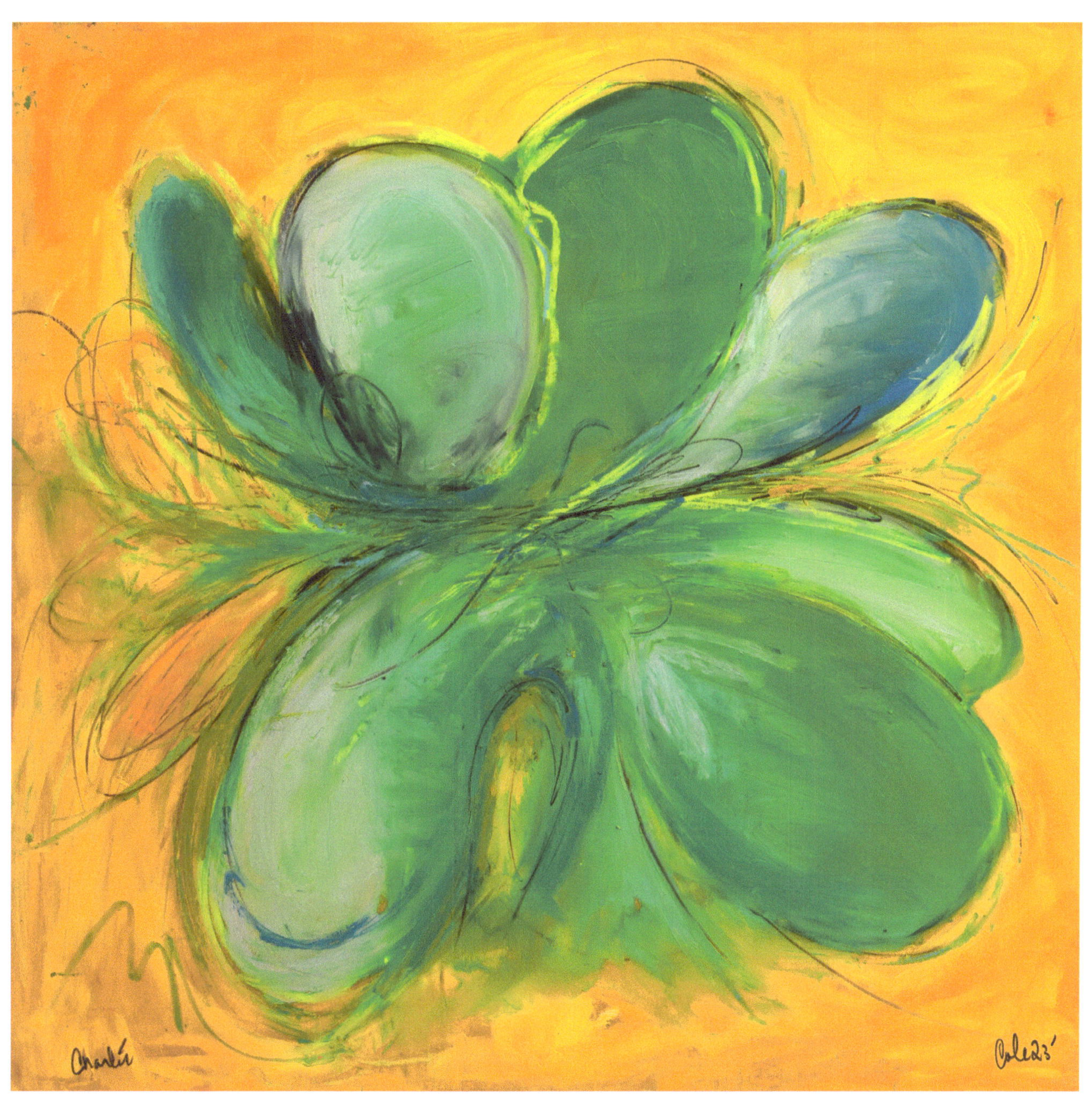

CRISSIE

Earth and Heaven Unite
20" x 20" oil on board

Hello, Dear Soul,

In your presence, earth and heaven
unite. Grounding roots hold the weight
of the kindness you extend to all

before you. Influenced by heaven,
your earthly existence is intense,
molding and shaping the children

before you. Souls touching,
you present in an asymmetrical
balance. Beautiful!

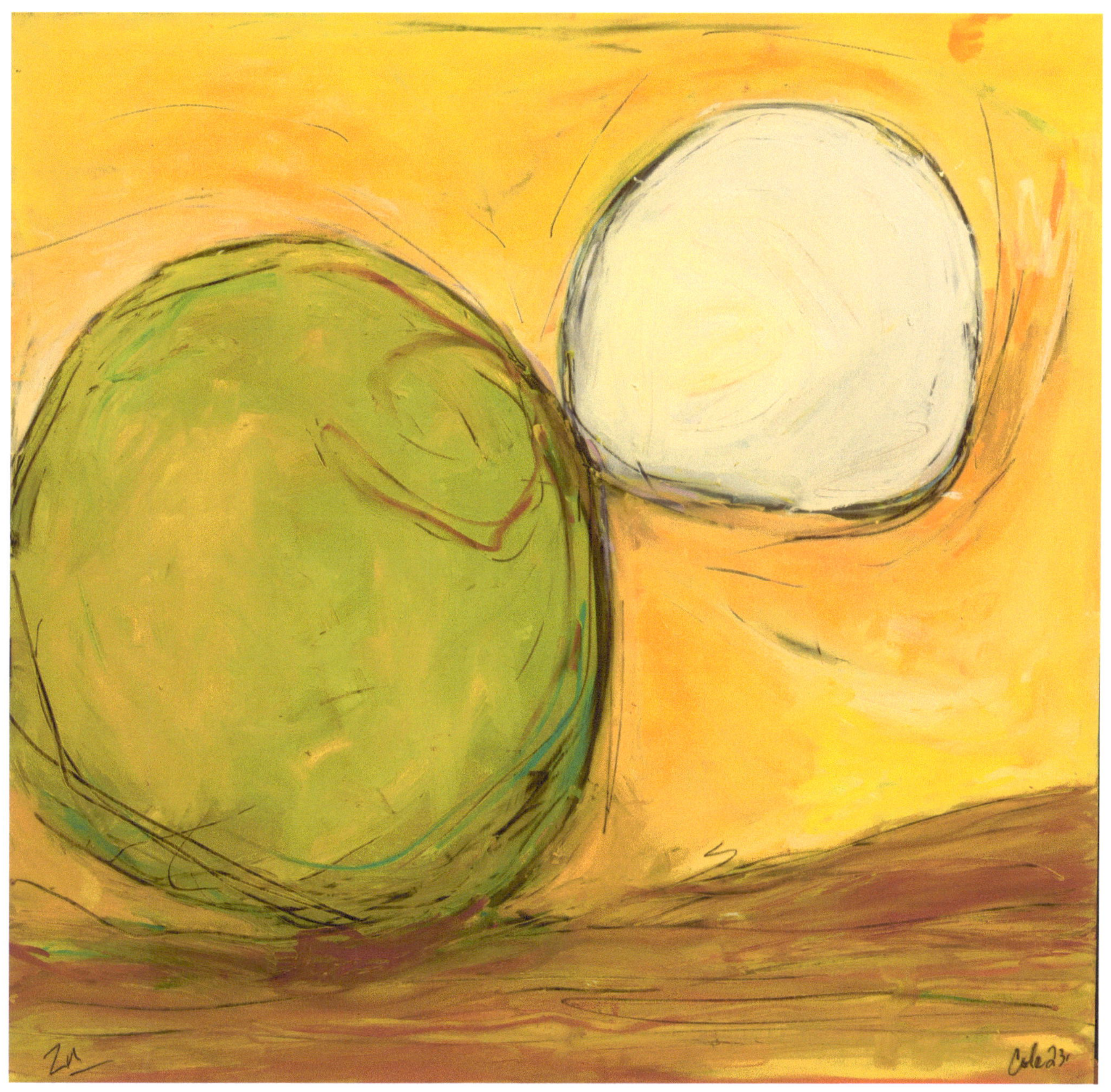

PEARL (canine)

Don't Stop
20" x 20" oil on board

Hello, Dear Soul,

You bounce and beam
with excitement. We learn to listen
to you heed the warning.

Deeply entrenched in your search
for adventure, we follow behind,

hoping - for a glimpse of your discovery.

Warmed by your strength and devotion,
we get in line to lift you up.

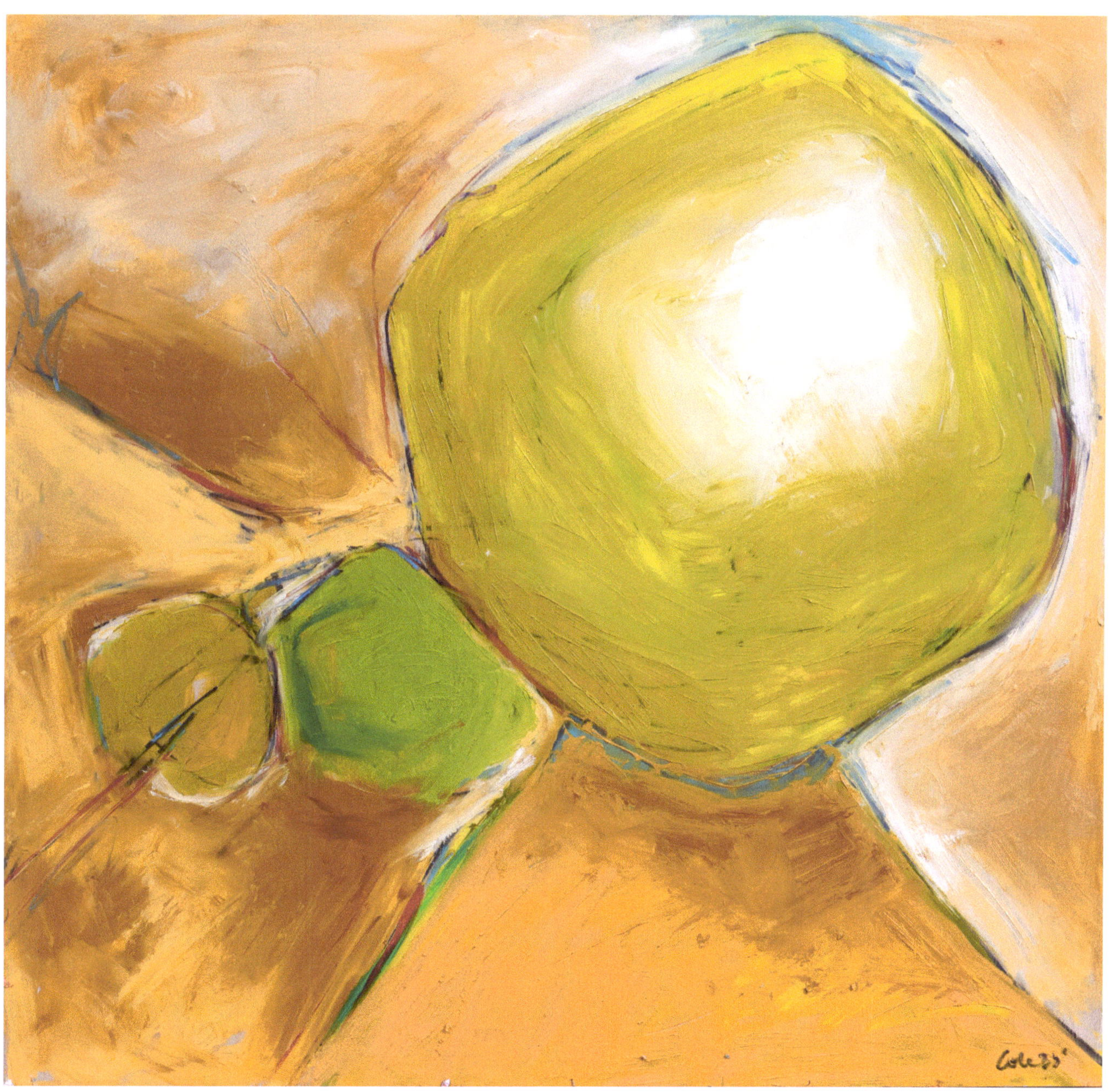

GENVIEVE

Gen's Rocket
20" x 20" oil on board

Hello, Dear Soul,

Pushing past any limitations,
you burst and surge to your chosen
destination, awaiting the word of mind
and body to believe in your dreams.

While supported by self with belief
in family, you round the earth.

Corner to corner, you lay down roots,
getting ready for everlasting longevity to create.

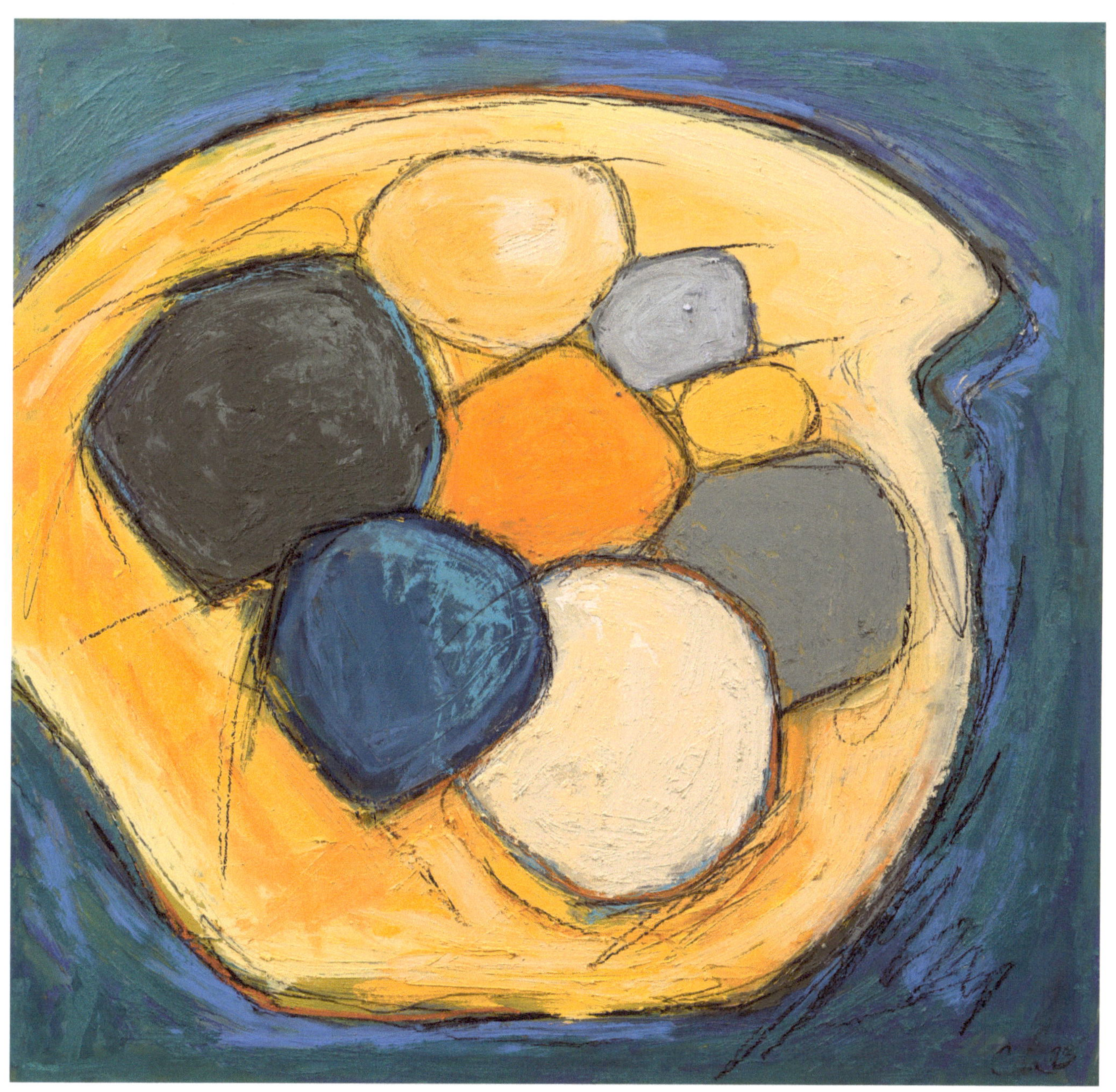

HEAVEN, SPACIOUSNESS

Interpretation of One Aspect of Heaven
20" x 20" oil on board

Hello, Dear Soul,

Focus on the clarity of light within you.

Allow that light to fill the open spaces
in your heart. Look for the blue of divinity

to wrap its loving arms around you.
Though it never left, your soul is home.

Peek behind the clouds; you will find us there
mingling about, awaiting your conversation.

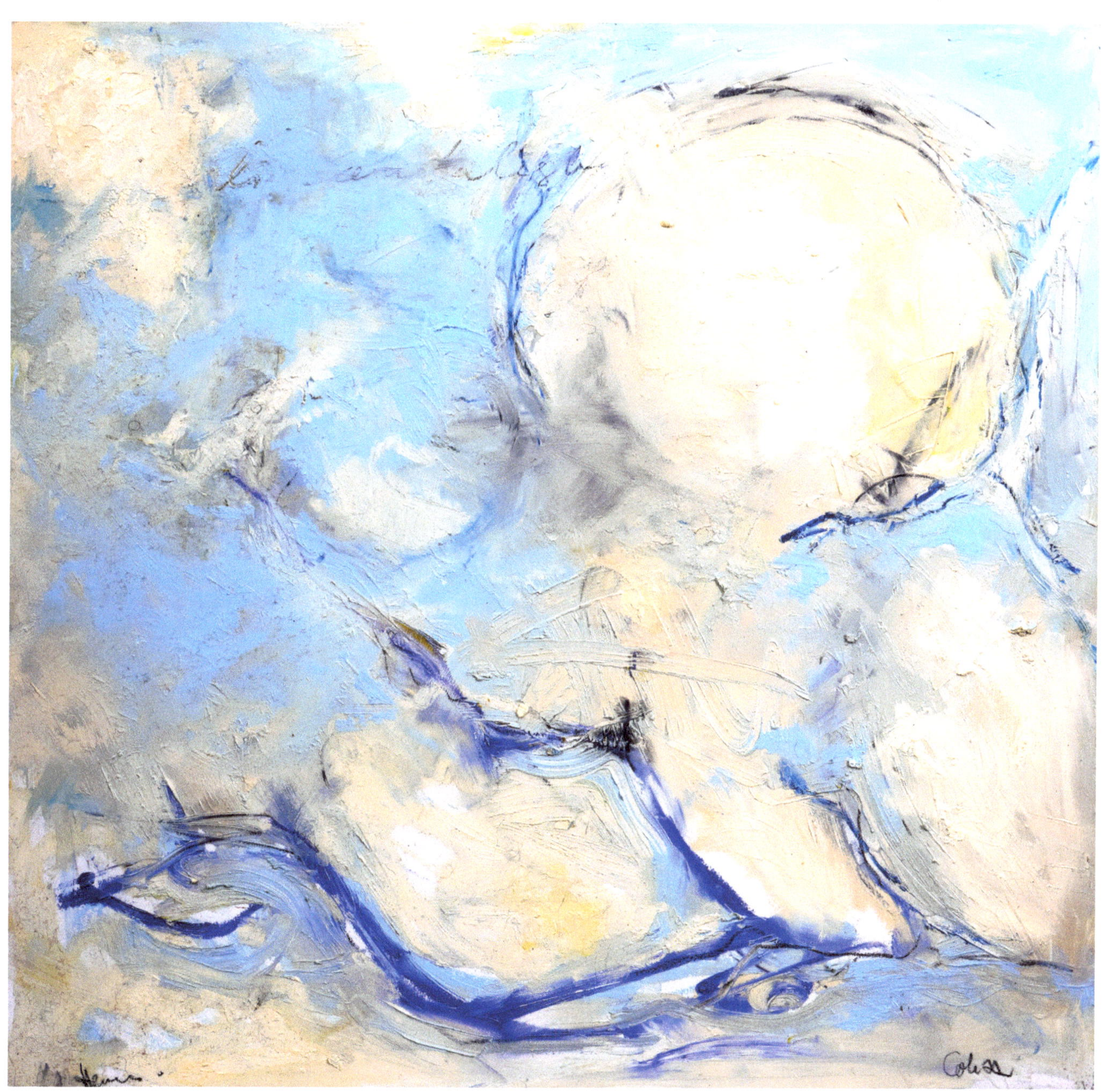

ROGER (Dad)

Hill and Dale
20" x 20" oil on board

Hello, Dear Soul,

Connected to animals, your communication
with them brings you peace and lasting friendship.

Why wouldnt it? You love all living creations,
dancing among them, singing and chirping in tune

like father, like daughter.

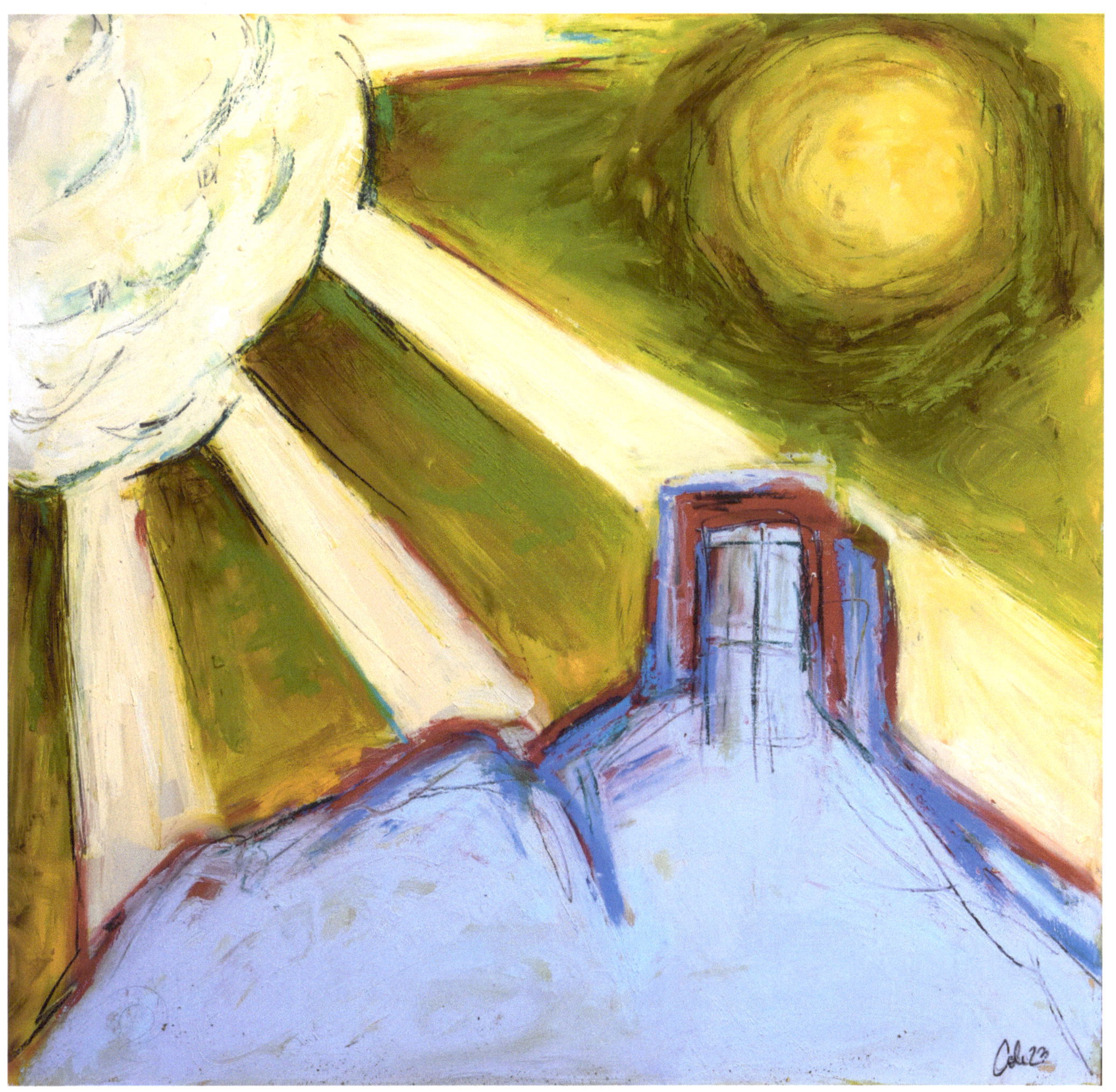

BOGART (canine)

Two-Sides
20" x 20" oil on board

Hello, Dear Soul,

Firm, confident, you stand fully grounded.
Roots dug in like colossal sequoias.

Balance of time and space,
you dazzle us with color, placement, and vibrancy.

You exude pure inextinguishable optimism.

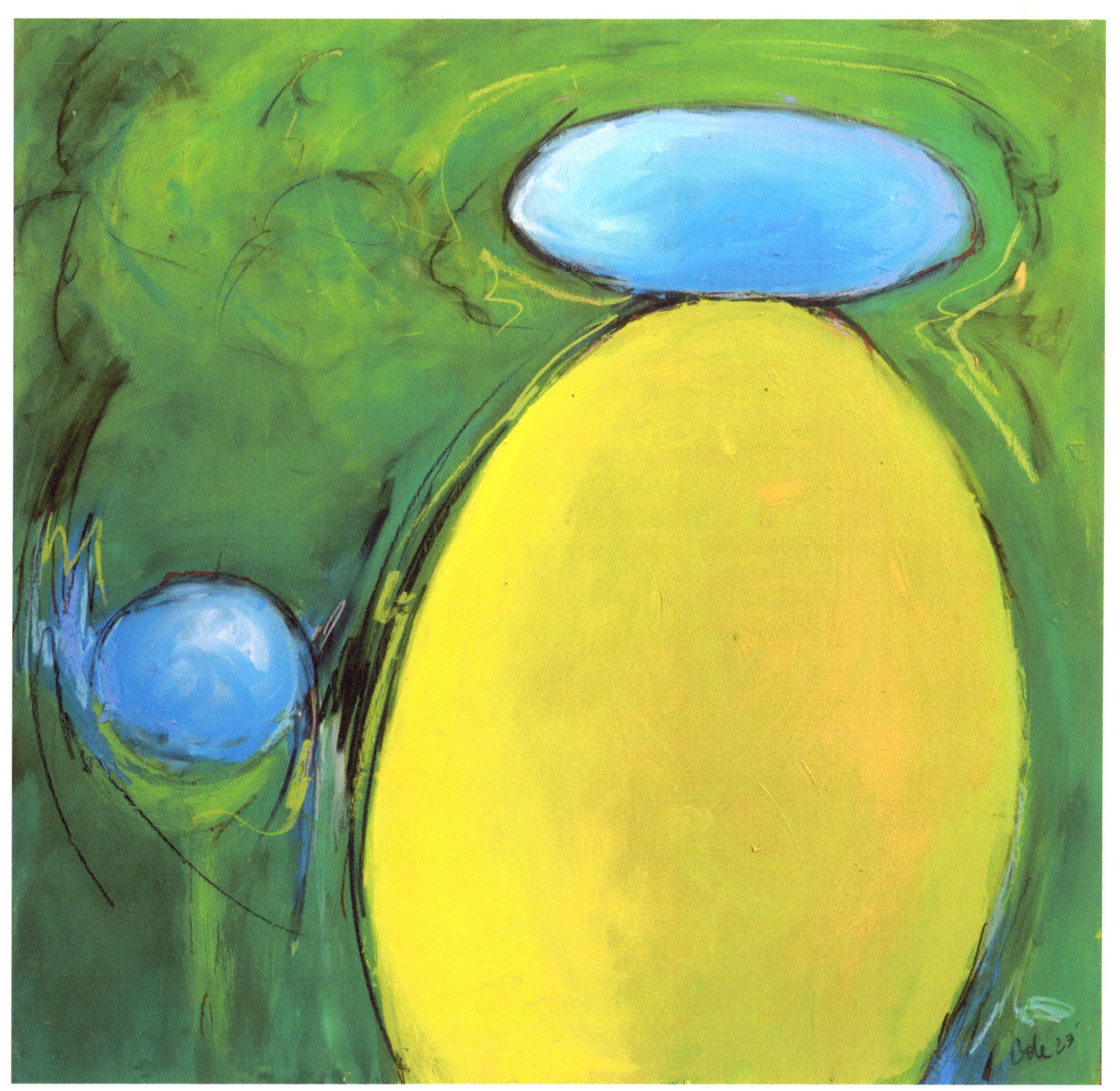

LUNA (canine)

Luna Love, Luna Light
20" x 20" oil on board

Hello, Dear Soul,

Golden sun, you are our light,
rising, setting to renew.

My best friend and confidant.
Hidden in the earth, surrounded by life,

you await the next mystery as our souls unite.

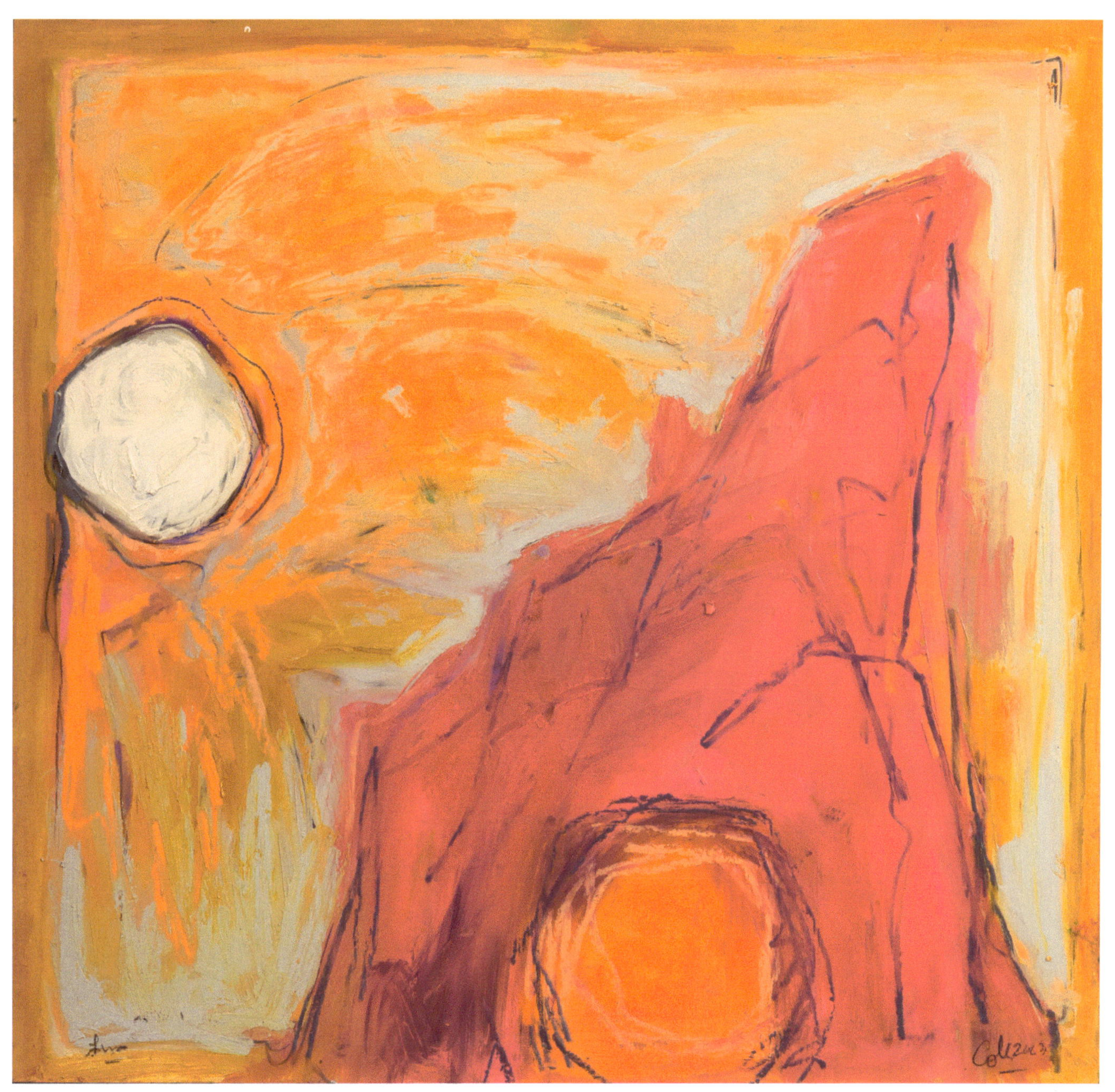

The Effects of Viewing One's Soul Painting

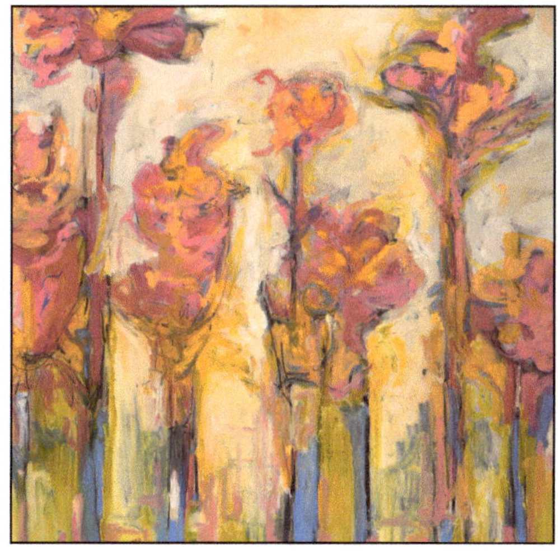

SOUL HEALING AND SOUL RETRIEVAL: Healing involves learning, growing, and changing. Change is constant, regardless of what we try to control. Deep concentration upon your soul painting will ignite the spark of self-inquiry and reveal fragments of your soul that may have been abandoned due to shame or neglect. From here, you can begin the process of retrieving them and nurturing them.

HEIGHTENED SELF-REFLECTION AND SELF-AWARENESS: Reflection and awareness are key to inner growth; therefore it is important to assess any messages you receive in the painting and then integrate the teachings. The colors and shapes will speak to you, prompting levels of honesty and contemplation never before accessed.

RECONDITIONING: Viewing your painting serves as a gateway to reconditioning, allowing the truths it speaks to undo a negative conditioned response and turn it into a positive and soul-affirming response. How do you do this? Through redirection. When you feel yourself starting to act out old patterns of behavior that no longer serve you, envision a stop sign and then pause. Catch yourself in the act and ask, "Is this my true nature, or is this an old pattern that is no longer serving me?" You can change the stories you tell yourself and form a new, more accurate self-image and self-belief—steeped in love, understanding, and trust.

A REKINDLED BELIEF IN YOUR ABILITIES: Allow your authentic sense of self and the confidence inspired by your soul painting to guide your actions. Do not second-guess your true essence. Challenge yourself to change the negative tape playing in your head from, "I can't do this" to "I *can* do this." Relearn a new version of yourself that is confident and expressive. Change can be hard. It takes intention, hard work, and discipline. But you can accomplish what you set out to do. Change involves making a conscious effort to do something different. Refrain from negative self-talk. If you do not accept this emotionally damaging treatment toward yourself, you will not accept it from others.

DEVELOP A CLOSER RELATIONSHIP WITH SOURCE: When you gaze upon your soul painting, there is a window of opportunity for the divine to touch you. When you open your heart and allow your imagination to flow freely, Source will speak through the shapes and colors. The messages are always loving, gentle, supportive, and serve to enhance your life by providing insight into your past, present, and future.

CREATE A TANGIBLE ROADMAP OF YOUR DREAMS: Your dreams, present or past, are a roadmap for consciousness itself. Your dreams are worlds of images, ideas, and colorful possibilities. What you believe is possible and informs your actions and intentions. Take your dream and add specificity and intention, then watch this visualization become your reality.

HEIGHTENED AWARENESS OF ONE'S ENERGY FIELD: Being in the presence of your soul painting will allow you to expand your energy field. Your energy frequency will match with the extraordinary passion and life radiating from your soul expression. Take a moment to be in reverence of this gift before you. When you vibrate at a higher frequency, your being will begin to transform.

UNDERSTAND YOUR CALLING: Many of us were taught who we were supposed to be and who we should love. Unfortunately, this tribal mindset strips us of authenticity and leaves many in fear of living a life outside of our family's dictates. It takes boldness to "color outside the lines." It takes faith to answer our soul's inner calling. When you view your soul painting, you will catch glimpses of potentials, and hear whispers of your true yearnings. This revelation is a blessing and should be thanked by answering the call.

RECEIVE CLARITY ON YOUR TALENTS AND GIFTS: Every individual needs a written or visual reminder of their diverse talents, gifts, and the extraordinary qualities they bring into this world. Viewing an abstract representation of these traits is like getting a divine download of tailor-made truth, inspiring your next steps to be fruitful.

EXPERIENCE A SURGE IN CREATIVITY: Everyone acts as a creator, even if traditional fine art is not their main expression. Creativity is in everything: gardening, cooking, teaching, decorating, writing, playing an instrument, fashion, acting, parenting, mentoring, entrepreneurship, and so on. Even how we fold our clothes and arrange them in the closet can be creative. Life is full of opportunities to express ourselves, but sometimes we get in a slump due to grief, trauma, depression, stress, and lack of confidence. Your soul painting can rekindle any dormant creativity so that it comes forth in the world, benefiting not only you but those you influence.

BECOME AN OBSERVER: Observing requires stillness and a nonjudgmental mind. When you observe your soul expression, it helps to open your heart and mind to the limitless potential before you.

EXPERIENCE YOUR SHADOW SIDE: Psychoanalyst Carl Jung developed the idea of the shadow self. While often referred to as dark and negative, our shadow side can be a positive force when brought into the light and understood: "The brighter the light, the darker the shadow."[5] Understanding your shadow side can help you identify hidden strengths or gain clarity over repressed emotions. Processing the shadow side gives you a clear perspective about the scope of your life's actions. What you make conscious can be an epiphany that changes your life. Imagine yourself sitting in the dark. If you simply turn on the light, consciousness reveals itself anew.

How to Interpret a Soul Painting

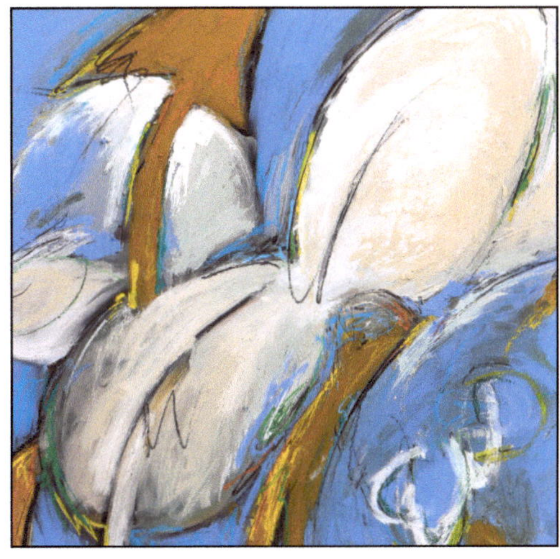

Soul paintings are one's emotional and energetic imprint translated onto the painting's surface. Set your soul painting in front of you. Sit with it for five minutes or so. What feelings arise when you look at it? Does it bring up specific memories? What do you see within the painting? What comes to mind in, around, and between the colors and marks on the surface? Study the colors and shapes. Is there a specific image coming forth? Feel into it. Abstract soul paintings often stir up a host of emotional responses: awe and wonder, emotional connection, curiosity, reflection, and contemplation.

Study the main colors of your soul, as well as the mark-making, complementary colors, express strokes, and solid areas interrupted by subtle changes in hues. Studying the perceived speed and direction of the marks tells you a lot about the energy of that soul. What energy do you get from the painting? Is it fast or slow? Closed or open? Each soul has a different emotional and energetic imprint that is unique to them. Souls that have already transitioned over have a higher level of openness and freedom with their expression. Now unencumbered, they have a newfound willingness to be boldly expressive without the fear and judgment that weighed down their earthly body. This boundless soul expression is unparalleled.

Practices to Open Your Heart, Intuition, and Creativity

INTENTIONALLY EXPERIENCE THE NATURAL WORLD

Spend time alone in the woods, filled with a variety of mosses, tall evergreens, lush maples, and sturdy sycamores. Or visit a body of water, such as a lake, pond, ocean, or even a delicate stream. As you take in the majestic beauty and awe around you, be mindful of your breath. Give yourself enough time alone to ponder the Universe and simply *be* with nature and animals. Be present by walking your dog with no distractions, no headphones, no phones. Keep bringing yourself back to your breath. Be in the present moment by sitting on the forest floor or the sand with your domestic animals: turtles, cats, dogs, rabbits, hamsters, anything with a nervous system. Take a ride out to the countryside and volunteer for the day on a farm, feeding and caring for farm animals and horses. Find your rightful path back to yourself and to life by being engaged with it.

MEDITATE

Meditation helps you to be the observer of your thoughts rather than the person who reacts. It allows you to pause in the space between your thoughts where peace is found. Meditation creates a space to take a mental break and can help reset your nervous system, calm your body, and soothe your soul. The practice of compassion, non-action, and contemplation is enhanced by regular meditation. The messages you get from spirit during these quiet times will light your way.

JOURNAL

Putting your thoughts down on paper can help you connect to spirit and, in turn, your true self. Journaling in the early morning or late evening is a good way to establish a regular routine. One unique and creative way to journal is through "automatic writing" to channel your soul's wisdom and tap into higher levels of consciousness. This practice also enhances intuition because you leave your logical mind behind during this practice.

BE PRESENT WITH YOUR ANIMAL FAMILY

Animals are pure love, pure joy. They are what humans aspire to be. What could be more evolved than that? To be in an animal's presence is God, prana, life, Source, Universe. They give us all these gifts if we are open to receiving and experiencing. We don't need to take a class and spend money to learn from our animals. All we need is to be open to possibilities and allow this unconditional love and joy to flow freely.

As you take a moment to be present with your animal companion, get on their level by getting down onto the ground. Notice your feet making contact with the ground as you lift your heart to the sky. Allow this exchange of love and joy to flow naturally through you. No distractions, just you and your companions. Notice that you are present, accepting and receiving unity and joy. Do this when possible three times a day. Your joy factor will increase exponentially. Simple and free . . . Just be.

GET CLEAR ON YOUR BELIEFS ABOUT DEATH TO REDUCE FEAR

Share your beliefs with a trusted friend or counselor regarding death, such as your doubts and fears about what happens when we transition out of the physical body, the world, or when we cross over. Decide what you believe regarding that transition. Energy is neither created nor destroyed; it is only transformed. We never cease to exist. How do you feel about this concept? Journal about it. You might enjoy reading Sherrie Dillard's book, *I'm Still with You,* on how to connect with your loved ones that have crossed over.[6] Learn how to pull their energy near you every day and visit with their spirit. Rest in the knowledge that your spirit team is supporting you from afar. There is comfort in knowing you are supported by others, whether or not they are physically present beside you. If you have anxiety, you probably enjoy being in your own quiet space without others. Nevertheless, there is a palpable energy of love and support that exists as connection, regardless of physical presence. Meaningful connection is always felt in our hearts.

ENGAGE IN MUSICAL PLAY FOR ENHANCED CREATIVITY

Do something creative to find your flow and quiet your chattering mind. Take up guitar and freely strum the chords with no plan or guidance. Think of your favorite song and feel the beat. Try to match it with no judgment. Feel the energy, speed, and tempo as you move up and down on the chords. Or make up your own song and beat; move up and down at your own speed. Listen and adjust your energy so you enjoy the sound. Make up your own rules, and have no expectations about the outcome. Do this daily, and be proud and present when you touch and feel the instrument: guitar, piano, drum, flute, violin, etc. Doing so allows you to trust the journey and the process as opposed to the destination or being tied to the outcome. Mostly, do this for you without care for what others think of you. Use this method of deconditioning with any creative endeavor: writing, dancing, singing, painting, and sculpting.

BE WARY OF OUTSIDE SOURCES

Psychic and mediumship readings can be helpful on your journey, but please get them from reputable sources. Those who share the essence of truth can serve as guideposts for your next steps. One helpful divination tool is a personalized astrology chart. Readings, communications, and astrology charts help validate what you are already feeling and know about yourself, emotionally and intuitively. Someone seeing and describing your beautiful light and essence that you came into the world to share helps you grow faster, allowing you to work through old patterns and move forward more confidently.

MAKE NO JUDGEMENTS

Every time you start to judge someone or a situation, take a moment to acknowledge that you have no idea what they have been through. The experiences they have endured influence why they are acting a certain way. Visualize your heart as a glowing ball of amber as love fills your heart space and your whole body. Send that glowing ball of positive, loving energy out to the person, the situation, and the world. Thank your heart for catching yourself in the act of judgment, and recognize its ability to feel deeply. Think of the people you love. Ask how you can become more accepting of others when they act in inappropriate ways or when they seem unconscious or unaware.

PRACTICE COMPASSION

Loss and grief can open your eyes to looking at the world differently, perhaps more inquisitively and compassionately. As you already know, it is not easy going through traumatic life events. But self-reflection during tragedy can open your eyes to the softness of the human soul. Grief and loss are shared human emotions that we can all relate to. The loss of a loved one can shatter you, like pieces of a puzzle, but through this raw, excruciatingly painful human experience, we become more human; we learn how to be more compassionate to others and ourselves.

ESTABLISH HEALTHY BOUNDARIES

Be aware of who and what you allow into your energy field and body—from food to books to movies to social media and the people you choose to spend time with. And don't forget those energy vampires! It's up to you to choose who you allow into your sacred space. Everyone can be negative from time to time. Life happens, and we all experience joyful highs and depressing lows. This is normal. But there are those who are chronically negative and feed on our good energy to survive emotionally. Be aware of these people, and keep your distance.

BE AWARE OF THE ENERGY FIELDS AROUND YOU

In the vein of energy vampires, it's important to have an awareness of the situations you put yourself in, especially if you are empathic. If you absorb others' emotions as a felt sense of physical agitation, notice how this feels inside your body. Shake out your arms and legs, or learn how to tap various points on the body (EFT) to work through triggers from past traumas. When your body is shaking from fear, or even the illusion of fear, EFT can work wonders. Tension in your muscles affects your well-being and your physical and emotional health. Learning to take care of yourself is an important part of growth, and this involves setting boundaries and protecting your energy field.

We have evolved throughout history by listening to our bodies, which never lie. If you feel tense or agitated in your body as you approach someone who is walking into an elevator, for example, listen. Do not get into that elevator. Your body can intuit safety and danger. It is an evolutionary trait that has allowed us to survive as a species.

Breathing Exercise for Grounding

Before I detail my deep-breathing technique, let me share why it's so beneficial. Deep breathing offers several benefits for both physical and mental well-being:

- *Stress Reduction:* Deep breathing activates the body's relaxation response, reducing stress and anxiety by stimulating the parasympathetic nervous system.

- *Improved Oxygen Flow:* Deep breaths increase the oxygen supply to your brain and body, promoting better circulation and overall health.

- *Enhanced Focus and Clarity:* It can improve concentration and cognitive function by increasing oxygen levels in the brain, helping you feel more alert and focused.

- *Lowered Blood Pressure:* Deep breathing can help reduce blood pressure by promoting relaxation and reducing the body's stress response.

- *Improved Respiratory Function:* It strengthens the diaphragm and increases lung capacity, which can be beneficial for people with certain respiratory conditions.

- *Detoxification:* Deep breathing supports the lymphatic system, aiding the body in removing toxins and waste.

- *Better Sleep:* Practicing deep-breathing techniques before bedtime can calm the mind and body, promoting better sleep quality.

- *Emotional Regulation:* It can help manage emotions by calming the nervous system and promoting a sense of tranquility.

To begin, sit in a comfortable posture. I like being in a quiet space. Breathe in and silently say, "I am." Hold your breath a few seconds, then exhale and say, "Calm." Repeat this four times. Visualize your breath moving throughout your body. Then picture your energetic body, which looks similar to your physical body, and watch the energy flowing from top to bottom and bottom to top. Open all of your primary seven chakras, from the ground up and then the top down (read further for detailed info on the chakra system). Spin them open, one at a time, then all the way up the body and all the way down your body, spinning all at once. Set an intention, or ask the Universe a question, and then quiet the mind. Look for an answer throughout your day. Notice the synchronicities all around you. There are no coincidences. Open your eyes to the beauty and magnificence of life itself.

CHAKRA MEDITATION FOR GROUNDING

Before I begin this exercise, let me give you a quick lesson on the chakra system and what it means to get the chakras "spinning" (balanced and active). The chakra system is a concept from ancient Indian spiritual traditions, particularly within yoga and Ayurveda. It describes a network of energy centers, or wheels, within the body, each associated with specific physical, emotional, and spiritual aspects. There are seven primary chakras aligned along the spine, from the base to the crown of the head. The chakra system suggests that when these energy centers are balanced and unblocked, they promote overall health and well-being. However, imbalances or blockages in these chakras might manifest as physical discomfort, emotional issues, or spiritual disconnect. Practices like yoga, meditation, breathwork, and energy healing aim to balance these chakras to promote harmony within oneself. As you go through this meditation, remember to focus on your deep breathing for optimal results.

ROOT CHAKRA (MULADARA): This is the first primary chakra (red), located at the base of the spine, and is responsible for your sense of security and stability. It is the base or foundation for life, and it helps you feel grounded and able to endure challenges. The root chakra embodies your sense of safety, which is why it is the foundation for all that follows. Noticing your feet on the ground is a powerful way of practicing grounding and becoming more aware of how connected we are to the earth, other sentient beings, and to life itself.

Readjust your position as you rock forward and backward, side to side. Shake out your arms and legs as you discharge angst or anxiety from your body. Notice your stance, and perhaps stand taller. Relax your shoulders. Your arms fall gently by your side. Breathe. Inhale peace. Exhale fear. When you are ready, wiggle your toes and press your bare feet into the earth. Feel how supported you are by nature, which is alive and always present, waiting to nurture and share its riches with you. Trees teach us about resilience and stability by being, not doing. One lesson we can learn from trees is how to live by standing tall with our roots grounding our being, knowing how strong we are. By doing less, you are accomplishing more. By being, not doing, you simply are. You are secure in this moment because you are in the present moment. And all we ever have is the present moment.

Visualize the color red flooding your body and the largest sequoia tree roots digging into the earth in all directions. Now spin your root chakra open. Visualization, according to brain science, is like actually being there. Imagine and it will be. See it clearly as if it has already happened, and it is done. Keep reminding yourself you are strong and grounded, like a tree. You are a beautiful part of the whole. You are secure, thriving, and safe.

SACRAL CHAKRA (SVADHISTHANA): This is the second primary chakra (orange) and is located below your belly button. It is responsible for how you experience sexuality, creative expression, and emotions. This chakra is also about your relationship with others and yourself. Are you able to express yourself and set boundaries? Are you having fun in life? Do you feel joy? Can you feel your feelings and express your desires clearly? Freedom of expression is part of having a sacral chakra that is in healthy alignment.

Visualize the color orange flooding your body. Envision the largest, ripest orange fruit you can imagine spilling out of the front, back, left, and right sides of your body. Spin your sacral chakra wide open. Breathe through your self-doubts. Honor the truth of who you are by allowing yourself to explore your creative, manifesting side.

SOLAR PLEXUS (MANIPURA): This chakra is the third primary chakra located in your navel area (yellow) and is associated with self-confidence, happiness, and joy. Having a strong solar plexus chakra will help you feel strong in your personal power, have a sense of knowing or "gut feeling," as well as a good sense of belonging. This chakra allows energy to flow freely, so if there is a blockage, emotional issues such as anger, irritability, and helplessness may be taking hold, and self-esteem may be low. Visualization can help you open your solar plexus chakra. Simply visualize a bright yellow lemon falling from the tree into your hands, and watch as yellow floods into your body on all four sides. Spin your solar plexus chakra left to open.

HEART CHAKRA (ANAHATA): This is the fourth primary chakra (green), located in the center of your chest, and is responsible for love and relationships, compassion, empathy, and forgiveness. Ahh . . . to be loved and to love. To be empathetic and compassionate toward yourself and others . . . This is the heart chakra. Like the color green in nature, deep and restful, the heart chakra also controls inner peace. Visualize pure green flooding your body—the deepest green pine tree or evergreen you can imagine. See green flooding in and out of your body. Spin your heart chakra open.

THROAT CHAKRA (VISHUDDHA): This the fifth primary chakra (blue) and is located in your throat. It is associated with speaking up and expressing yourself, finding your voice, hearing, and being heard. Visualize the color blue flooding your body, the bluest skies you've ever witnessed, or the coolest ocean waters you have ever felt. Soak in the refreshing sensations of blue water as you spin your throat chakra open.

THIRD EYE CHAKRA (AJNA): This is known as the "mind's eye" and is the sixth primary chakra, located at the forehead between the eyes (indigo). It is associated with intuition, insight, and mysticism. It controls the meridian of the body, mind, and spirit. Picture the color indigo flooding your body as you spin your sixth chakra open.

CROWN CHAKRA (SAHASRARA): This is the seventh primary chakra and is located at the top of your head (violet or light purple) and represents our connection to our higher power, the self, and the divine, as well as transformation. Visualize the color purple flooding your body and spin your crown chakra open.

As you went through the chakra meditation, what did you notice in your energy field with each chakra spinning? Perhaps your breath provided a clear, cool sensation mimicking a waterfall or a lake. Let it flow forward as you release stuck energy from the past. Inhale. Exhale.

Exercises to Stimulate Creativity

These exercises can work for creating anything: art, writing, choreographing fluid dance moves, making music, etc. For example, if you want to paint what you feel, first ground yourself in the present moment. Notice your feet on the ground and then breathe. If you have anxiety, depression, or PTSD, it may be challenging to clear your mind. Repetitive negative thoughts may be circulating throughout your mind, and you may feel helpless to stop them. Take a moment to notice that your mind is racing. Without judgment, acknowledge the present moment without trying to change anything. Take a deep breath in, then a long breath out.

If your body feels agitated, try shaking out your arms and legs, then go for a walk or run. If you are anxious, focusing on breathing may not be a great choice at this moment. You may choose physical movement instead. Discharging some of the agitation in your body might be what you need. Awareness and acceptance lead the way toward understanding, so simply allow the process to unfold. Accept the present moment as it is; let it be. There is peace in knowing you are safe in this moment, allowing everything to be exactly as it is. No resistance, just awareness.

IMMERSE YOURSELF IN THE ENERGY OF PAINTING

Get your mind right: "Spirit is the life, mind the builder and physical is the result."[7] Imagine what it might feel like to love yourself completely. We are conditioned by society not to feel our emotions. We are told to be positive and keep negativity to ourselves. But false positivity is harmful. It is the opposite of authenticity and self-acceptance. It is pretending or having a facade we show to the world as we stuff our sadness, frustration, and anger. What is wrong with owning and sharing what we feel? If you feel sad, then cry! Tell people you feel sad. Own your sadness. Who is to say it is not okay to show raw emotions? Isn't it more authentic and inspiring to be real? You can't heal if you don't feel.

The right people will have compassion and support you when you express your emotions. Yes, even if they are sad emotions. The others . . . Well, you don't care about them anyway. They are not your people. Be yourself. In this world, we need your authenticity. Your unique talents are needed. Your smile, your laugh, and your goodness are valued. This world needs your light. So be bold and be you. Channel, or let flow, the emotions onto the artistic surface. Now you are ready to create.

Intention: Setting an intention to create is the first step. Ask yourself: "What would I like to create?" Is there meaning in your creative endeavor? Would you like to dedicate your work to someone you love? Or do you want to create with purpose to unleash your unique gifts into the world? Do you have a motive, or is this creativity for pleasure? Inhale peace. As you exhale, let go of judgment. Let go of how you think things should be. Accept the present moment as it is. I know sometimes it is difficult to accept yourself exactly as you are, but in this moment, try.

We can do it together.

Notes

1. Eric R. Kandel, "Reductionism in Art and Brain Science: Bridging the Two Cultures,"
   The Diatrope Institute, Nov. 28, 2021, https://diatrope.com/kandel-reductionism-art-brain/.
2. Eric R. Kandel, "Abstract Art and the Brain," Master & Dynamic, April 3, 2017,
   https://www.masterdynamic.com/blogs/sounds-selects/abstract-art-and-the-brain.
3. Eric R. Kandel *Reductionism in Art and Brain Science: Bridging the Two Cultures,*
   Columbia University Press; Illustrated edition (August 30, 2016).
4. Julie Mehretu, Brainy Quote, https://www.brainyquote.com/quotes/julie_mehretu_536031.
5. Carl Jung, Pacifica Graduate Institute, https://pacifica.libguides.com/Jung/shadow#:~:
   text=Jung%20 was%20well%20aware%20of,shadow%20which%20makes%20us%20human.%22.
6. Sherrie Dillard, *I'm Still with You: Communicate, Heal, and Evolve with Your Loved One on
   the Other Side* (Llewellyn Publishers, Minnesota) 2020.
7. Edgar Cayce quote, "Cayce Key Concepts," Edgar Cayce's A.R.E of California,
   https://www.edgarcayceca.org/edgar-cayce/cayce-concepts/.

About the Author

Nicole is a lifelong artist and designer with a graphic design degree from Virginia Commonwealth University in Richmond, Virginia. She has spent most of her career as an abstract painter and educator, balancing the functions of text and image in her artwork. Her experience ranges from solo shows to large environmental installations, most revolving around earth, nature, and animals. Presently, Nicole's work has evolved into a multifaceted career as an animal communicator and painter of souls. Her dual calling allows her to reach and help heal clients all over the world.

You can listen to interviews with her through various metaphysical podcasts, such as *Enlightened Empaths Podcast, Skeptic Metaphysicians, Sense of Soul Podcast, Intuition Talks, Connection to the Cosmos, Soul Traveler, Reluctant Medium, Spirit Talk,* and *Edgar Cayce's New Awakenings.* You can also follow her work at Nicoleharp.com, Harpspace.org, Instagram: @harpspace, and YouTube.

When Nicole is not working, she can be found spending time with her rescue animals and spouse. Nicole spends as much time as she can in the studio healing through painting the energy of nature, humans, and animals, living or that have crossed over.

Readers can find out more about ordering their own soul painting or commission one for a loved one, animal, or human at Harpspace.org.

Acknowledgments

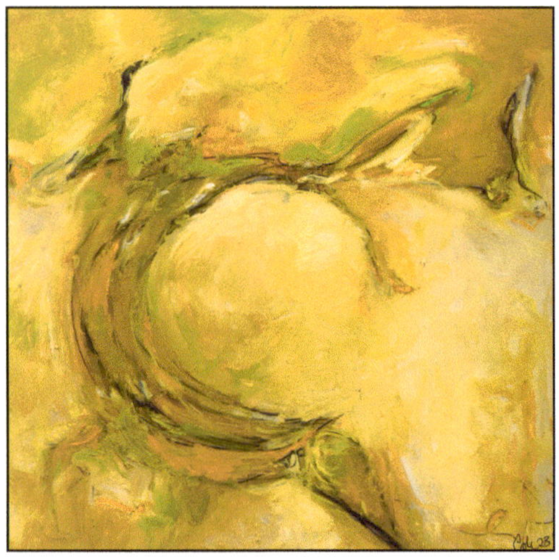

Being a caregiver for someone you love is difficult, but to care for a perfect stranger as if they were your family is a gift and a calling. It takes a level of compassion few humans possess. I am immensely grateful to Indira Samaroo, Kathy Corley, Roxanne Moore, Anni Veyo, and Monica and Jim Flynn, who treated my mother with dignity, respect, and kindness during the dying process. Thank you for holding my mother's hand and mine so I could face another day.

To Amy Wheeler, my spouse and best friend, who knows me better than I know myself. You taught me how to cry and how to feel my heart in my body.

Thank you to Jenna Love Schrader, my copy editor and insightful sounding board.

Thank you to Susan Joy Rizman, my friend who is like a sister.